D0934164

PUBLICATIONS
OF THE FACULTY OF ARTS
OF THE UNIVERSITY OF MANCHESTER
No. 25

TRAWTHE AND TREASON

The sin of Gawain reconsidered

To the memory of
Eugène Vinaver

TRAWTHE AND TREASON

The sin of Gawain
reconsidered

❀

A thematic study of
Sir Gawain and the Green Knight

W. R. J. BARRON

MANCHESTER
UNIVERSITY PRESS

© W. R. J. BARRON 1980

Published by
MANCHESTER UNIVERSITY PRESS
Oxford Road, Manchester M13 9PL

Distributed in the USA by Barnes and Noble Books
81 Adams Drive, Totowa, N.J. 07512

ISBN 0 7190 1294 5

BRITISH LIBRARY CATALOGUING IN PUBLICATION DATA

Barron, William Raymond Johnston
    Trawthe and treason. – (University of Manchester.
    Faculty of Arts. Publications; no. 25).
    1. Sir Gawain and the Green Knight
    I. Title   II. Series
    821'.1   PR2065.G3

ISBN 0–7190–1294–5

Phototypeset by
Western Printing Services Ltd, Bristol
Printed in Great Britain by
The Pitman Press, Bath

CONTENTS

PREFACE

Yet another interpretative study of *Sir Gawain and the Green Knight*! One might have thought that the degree of thematic consensus reflected in the 1965 studies by Benson and Burrow was sufficient basis for the critical work which is properly our concern. But the torrent of commentary and analysis has swollen rather than slackened in the interim, implying the impossibility of separating the study of method and meaning, and showing how richly harmonised the poem is, many literary subtleties emerging as the thematic outline is filled in more fully. Who can say that the process has been completed?

Recent publications have been persistently concerned with certain areas and aspects of the text, suggesting continuing uncertainty about the relationship of the parallel indoor and outdoor scenes in the third fitt, the precise nature of the fault committed by Gawain, and the bearing upon it of his two confessions: 'The relation between the hunts and the indoor games has never adequately been explained; and we have been the losers in trying to decide what rule Gawain broke or indeed whether he won or lost.'[1] Reading recent studies, and re-considering much that had appeared earlier, I have been led to see the hunting as having an interpretative bearing, complex and shifting, upon the indoor games of wooing and wagering, and as compelling judgement and offering guidance on the nature of Gawain's fault. The effect has been to give structural and thematic meaning to elements in the poem hitherto considered purely incidental, to show that the twin plots, Beheading and Temptation, are even more essentially interrelated than had been supposed, and to add an element of precision to the moral import of the whole.

But why at such length? Though I believe the interpretation offered is in general accord with received opinion, there are some startling suggestions which I owe it to myself to establish in sufficient detail to win conviction. Further, some are rooted in medieval social, legal, and theological usages whose literary relevance raises issues of interpretation:

Parallels in contemporary background can generally be found for any interpretation of any work, so that to claim that a reading has 'historical support' has no probative value. Historical background is so various that unless an interpretation is particularly eccentric some degree of overlap is inevitable. By the same token, it is an equally illicit procedure to begin with one element in a complex cultural context and apply it only to those parts of a work which correspond.[2]

But it would surely be perverse to imagine that medieval poetry can safely be interpreted in complete disregard of the beliefs and practices of the society in which and for which it was written. Even such an idealistic form as the romance clothed its fictions in the trappings of the day, endowing its chivalric golden age not only with medieval manners, dress, and architecture but with the social structure and legal usage of feudalism, many of its cultural attitudes and patterns of thought, much of its system of beliefs, Christian and mythic.

Our own knowledge of such matters is often incomplete, always second-hand, and – more seriously – formal and technical, learnt from codes and handbooks rather than absorbed from life. We know them in a form which allows us to recognise a technical reference, but not as unconsciously assimilated elements of a total culture which would allow us to identify them automatically as parts of a complex literary structure, alluded to obliquely, perhaps ironically inverted, given metaphorical or allegorical significance, or evoked in terms of their associated values, moods, and atmospheres rather than concretely. We recognise the economic importance of hunting in the Middle Ages, but can we, despite its still potent survival, comprehend its full significance for a society which surrounded it with sacrosanct ceremonial, a whole corpus of law, and a literature both technical and moral? Can we fully appreciate the extent to which personal knowledge of the law was a matter not only of feudal obligation and self-interest but of the daily preoccupations of a ruling class which really ruled? Can we feel the full fascination of theology for laymen to whom it represented not only the way to personal salvation but God's design for his universe, attested by every aspect of the world around them?

The technical establishment of such aspects of social context demands space; consideration of their conventional literary formulation, even in the imperfect way which the present limitations of our knowledge allow, demands still more. And if the evidence which this material offers is not to be misused by the kind of 'template criticism' which erects one identification or interpretation into a ruling concept, ignoring everything which cannot be read in conformity with it, space is needed to demonstrate its validity in the wider context of the work. I have tried to fit my ideas into a detailed reading of the text, and to indicate, wherever possible, how they conform to or conflict with those of other scholars. In the process I have sought to adduce meaning rather than impose it, and to remember always that:

... the meaning, or meanings, in a complex work of art are virtually inexhaustible, and, it goes without saying, utterly irreducible to a flat statement or to prose. That is why, since it is organic without being substantial, architectonic without being architectural, and systemic without being systematic, the literary art object has baffled and beaten interpreters who seize upon it as a cryptogram to be deciphered, rather than as an ordered structure to be directly known. To fumble with the ill-fitting keys of biography, history, antiquarianism or any other partial 'philology' that seduces immediate attention from the text, reduces one to peeping squinteyed through the keyhole with the vision distorted and foreshadowed. That is always the temptation: to pragmatise the poem, to read into it, or out of it, instead of contemplating it wholly.[3]

If, having imposed on my readers at such length, my ideas cannot command imaginative conviction, their historical validity will not save them from oblivion; if they are in conformity with the artistic integrity of the poem, they will in time impose themselves.

I am deeply indebted to my colleague Dr J. J. Anderson and to Dr R. A. Waldron who, by their perceptive and kindly criticism, have saved me from many errors of imbalance and over-enthusiasm. For those which no doubt still exist, I must take personal responsibility. My thanks are also due to Manchester University Press, in particular to John Banks as editor, for their care in the reproduction of the text.

NOTES

1   D. R. Howard in *Recent Middle English Scholarship and Criticism: Survey and Desiderata* (ed. J. Burke Severs), Pittsburg, Pa., 1971, pp. 42–3.

2   Edward Wilson, *The Gawain-Poet*, Leiden, 1976, p. 117.

3   Ralph Baldwin, *The Unity of The Canterbury Tales* (*Anglistica* V), Copenhagen, 1955, p. 12.

I HUNTING AND WOOING

The third fitt of *Sir Gawain and the Green Knight* is the most consciously structured and elaborately patterned unit in the work of one of the most form-conscious of all English poets. He has clearly been at pains to set its action apart from the rest of the poem; supplying all narrative essentials before it begins, suspending Gawain's anxiety as to the whereabouts of the Green Chapel, establishing the Exchange of Winnings compact casually in the festive context of Christmas games, dismissing the other guests on the previous evening so that for the last three days of his stay at Hautdesert the hero remains alone with his hosts. For that period the action of the poem seems suspended: the fitt opens and closes with Gawain in his bed, where, voluntarily and involuntarily, he passes much of its duration. The interval is filled with a series of games, hunting, *luf-talkyng*, and the Exchange of Winnings, ordered with the easy formality of established convention in an atmosphere of courtly relaxation. The structure of the fitt reproduces the superficial formality of games – three days, three hunts, three wooings, three exchanges, while its rhetoric involves repeated patterns of potential symbolic value – three hunted animals, three kisses, three love-tokens (glove, ring and girdle), three visits to the castle chapel. And its dominant mood is one of civilised order and good breeding, with laughter and social badinage between intimates.

But these impressions are superficial. On reflection and re-reading, the mood seems ominously undercut by uncertainty and disorder, violence and cruelty without and unspoken threat within, the familiar, vigorous ritual of the hunt oddly at variance with the unhealthy stasis of the love-game in the bedroom, obscure in motivation and implication. The very regularity of the structural and rhetorical patterns raises doubts. What is the symbolic significance – if any – of the animals hunted? Can the girdle be equated with the other love-tokens; is it proffered and accepted in the same spirit? Is there some significant connection between the hunting and the wooing? Even the familiar folklore rhythm of repeated threes is unreassuring, since in folk tales the pattern is so often broken on the third repetition. So, in retrospect, this interval of restful recuperation may well appear a vital testing time for the hero, its inactivity concealing the central and crucial action of the poem, vaguely sensed even at first reading. And its apparent isolation from the rest of the action is illusory: Gawain's continuing awareness of the impending blow at the Green Chapel distracts him in his amorous fencing with the Lady and troubles his sleep, while the outcome of the Exchange of Blows contest will prove to depend upon that apparently superficial social duel between them, the triple pattern of the one impinging on the twin structure of the other. These contradictions, ambiguities and inherent ironies inevitably condition interpretation even of the most concrete details.[1]

Nothing could be more concrete than the temporal relationship which the poet has created between the hunting and the bedroom scenes. By carefully noting the hour of Bertilak's departure for the field (*By þat any dayly3t lemed vpon erþe* (1137)), following him throughout the day *to þe derk ny3t* (1177) before switching back to the castle where Gawain still lies abed, *Lurkkez quyl þe dayly3t lemed on þe wowes* (1180), remaining with him *al day, til þe mone rysed* (1313) before returning to the hunters *bi þat þe sunne heldet* (1321) and bringing them back home *Bi þat þe dayly3t watz done* (1365), he contrives to suggest that the action in both locations occurs simultaneously.[2] The thematic significance of this simultaneity on the third day has been widely recognised; that it also has functional significance on the earlier days seems probable.

What that function might be cannot even be guessed at before the end of the first day. The opening of the deer hunt might therefore suggest to the reader merely a continuation of those seasonal festivities which occupied the end of the previous fitt, material of incidental and technical interest designed to display the poet's descriptive powers. This is certainly how modern critics initially interpreted all the hunting scenes, and their vividness, technical accuracy and ability to engage the attention justify such an approach. But our increasing awareness of the strict economy of the poem suggests that nothing in it is merely ornamental or incidental and that the casual function of a passage may conceal a more fundamental organic purpose. Here, as elsewhere, the rhetorical treatment, the emotional overtones, the atmosphere evoked may be more significant guides to function than the factual content. Factually the deer hunt (1133–77, 1319–68) is characterised by meticulous adherence to contemporary practice, accurate use of technical vocabulary and an overall impression of good order, of aristocratic *savoir faire* and due procedure which the court of Bertilak shares with Camelot.[3] But the modern reader, identifying less immediately than the original courtly audience with the 'world' of the poem, may be more conscious of presentation than technical content.

The opening movement of the deer hunt, up to the Lady's entrance into Gawain's bed-chamber, falls into two sections divided by the stanza break at line 1149. The first is concerned exclusively with the hunters, expresses a spirit of robust vigour in men and dogs, and conveys it largely in terms of sound: *bugle*; *calde*; *Blwe bygly in buglez þre bare mote*; / *Braches bayed þerfore and breme noyse maked*; *Þer ros for blastez gode* / *Gret rurd in þat forest*. The ambiguity of *rurd* – possibly the noise of the hunt, more probably the panic of the hunted (*cf*. OED *rerd(e)* n., 2(b)) – prepares the transition to a second section built on continuity and contrast: continuity in the orderly procedure of the hunt and the use of sound to convey its effect; contrast in that the narrative is now with the hunted deer and the sounds are as perceived by them, the terrifying signs of encirclement and pursuit: *þe fyrst quethe of þe quest*; *þe stablye, þat stoutly ascryed*; *halden in with hay! and war!*; *dryuen with gret dyn*; *wapped a flone*; *Hunterez wyth hyȝe horne*; *Wyth such a crakkande kry as klyffes haden brusten*. The sound continuum links natural cataclysm and human passion, the terror of the driven beasts and the excitement of man the hunter. The latter re-emerges to dominate the end of the hunt and the day closes in the mood of exaltation with which it opened:

> Þe lorde for blys abloy
> Ful oft con launce and lyȝt,
> And drof þat day wyth joy
> Thus to þe derk nyȝt.   (1174-7)

Despite the difficulty of judging a medieval intention from a modern response, the intended effect of the passage is surely one of emotional ambiguity which leaves the reader unsure of what his reaction should be. Led by the rhetorical procedure to expect a set-piece of courtly living, like so many in Fitt II, he finds himself induced, naturally and acceptably, to associate with the delight of the hunters and, by the same sharply evocative means, with the terror of the hunted. Medieval readers, for whom the natural order was man-centred, might find the latter reaction abnormal and unnatural but surely irresistible in response to such vivid and emotive writing:

> Þe hindez were halden in with hay! and war!
> Þe does dryven with gret dyn to þe depe sladez;
> Þer myȝt mon se, as þay slypte, slentyng of arwes –
> At vche wende vnder wande wapped a flone –
> Þat bigly bote on þe broun with ful brode hedez.
> What! þay brayen, and bleden, bi bonkkez þay deȝen
>   (1158-63)

The ambivalence evoked by this treatment of the deer hunt would, I suggest, be only vaguely perceptible, an uneasiness as to the expected response, until activated by the parallelism of the first bedroom scene.[4] Recent research has begun to establish that that parallelism exists at emotional and atmospheric levels as much as in narrative details. As the narrative and rhetorical patterning of the bedroom scenes has been exhaustively analysed, my purpose here is to bring out those aspects of the interrelationship in which emotional response is most operative.

I would suggest that the basis of the interrelationship, at many levels, is continuity and contrast. There is obvious superficial continuity in the opening lines of the first bedroom scene (1178-81), reminding us how Gawain has lain *Vnder couertour ful clere, cortyned aboute* since, the previous night, he was conducted with all ceremony (1119–21) to his bed *ful softe*, in a chamber whose luxury has already been described (852–9) in terms which recall the material splendours of his own court of Camelot (*cf.* 75–80). Indeed, since his arrival there, Hautdesert has repeatedly been described in ways which evoke memories of Arthur's court: as a place of courteous welcome (807–41; *cf.* 250–78), presided over by a worthy lord (842–9; *cf.* 53–7, 85–9); a place of ordered ceremony (995–1009; *cf.* 72–80, 109–115), where religious duties are duly observed in chapel (927–40; *cf.* 62–5) and Christmas properly celebrated with feasting (884–98; *cf.* 116–28), music (1014–15; *cf.* 116–20) and wine (977–80, 1025; *cf.* 129) – perhaps to excess (899–900; *cf.* 497–9); a place whose seasonal sports include mimic contest (981–90; *cf.* 41–3) and a game of forfeits involving an equal exchange between the contestants (1105–15; *cf.* 66–70,[5] 283–98). The implications of this congruity are, presumably, that Gawain has merely exchanged one Camelot for another and can sleep secure in the comfort of a household whose members observe the standards and, to all appearance, share the values of Arthur's court. But the implications may be uncomfortably ambivalent for readers who have felt those values slighted by events at Camelot before Gawain's departure: the shocked silence of a court whose *glaum ande gle* is hushed by a challenger who appears as if in fulfilment of Arthur's festive usage, undertaken *þur3 nobelay*, and seems at first to demand no more than the customary response (275–8; *cf.* 96–9); the intemperance of a king, admirably *3ep*, yet *sumquat childgered*, who *wex as wroth as wynde* and responded impulsively to a challenge which he had judged *nys* and *foly* (McClure, p. 382); the hypocrisy of his followers who, having corporately advised *To ryd þe kyng wyth croun, / And gif Gawan þe game* (364–5), later criticise him behind his back for exposing Gawain to a fate which they had not themselves foreseen:

> '. . . britned to no3t,
> Hadet wyth an aluisch mon, for angardez pryde.
> Who knew euer any kyng such counsel to take
> As kny3tez in cauelaciounz on Crystmasse gomnez!'
>
> (680–3)

Camelot, it would seem, has, under test, fallen short of the high repute which brought the test upon it (258–64).[6] In so far as Hautdesert appears another Camelot, can its adherence to Christian and chivalric values under test, the innocence of its drinking and its festive games, its security as a resting place for an unarmed knight, be taken for granted? Will the ominous outcome of the seasonal sports at Camelot prove to have any bearing on those played at Hautdesert? Is the Exchange of Winnings compact there to be equated with the light-hearted contention over the *ȝerez-ȝiftes* at Arthur's court, or with the deadly Exchange of Blows compact couched in the same legal terminology?[7] Can the impeccable *cortaysye* which brought Gawain through the events at Camelot without displaying either the intemperance of Arthur or the cowardice and duplicity of his fellow knights, with humility in taking up the challenge (343–61) and without recrimination when it proved so disastrous (545–9), sustain his reputation in this other Camelot?

At the same time, there are contrastive elements in the presentation of Hautdesert which inhibit identification with Camelot. The four stanzas (36–129) and the generalised vocabulary (*luflych*, *rych*, *oryȝt*, *gentyle*, *dere*, *louelokkest*, *comlokest*, *fayre*, *hapnest*, etc.) given to the latter inevitably contrast with the half fitt (763–1125) of detailed, evocative description, constantly changing perspective, and close scrutiny which establish the former. Camelot is presented with the vagueness of conventional romance, in terms of its established reputation and traditional usages; Hautdesert with detailed realism of setting, architecture, personal description, formal ceremony and boisterous sport, intimate conversation and private thoughts very unusual in romance and remarkable in the strict economy of *Sir Gawain*. The implication, presumably, is that this society is to play such a vital role in the scheme of the poem that its people must be intimately known and, to a degree, socially identified with the contemporary audience. Yet there is an element in its presentation which undermines the concreteness and inhibits the reader's association with the world of Hautdesert. Gawain's approach to the castle (691–702), out of the romance realm of Logres, through the concrete geography of North Wales, the fords across the sands of Dee, the notorious wilderness of Wirral, brings him towards the homeland of the north-west midlands audience, along a mapped route familiar to them (Waldron, p. 61), where such grotesques as the Green Knight are unknown (703–8). But beyond Wirral he passes back into *contrayez straunge* (708–62), where the conventional adventures of romance crowd upon him in a breathless catalogue, and creatures of romance, *wormez*, *wodwos* and *etaynez*, mingle with the native fauna, *wolues*, *bullez* and *borez*, in the tangled forests and bitter winter weather of the north. In this godless land (701–2), Mary's knight is still in God's hand (724–5), and at his prayer for shelter in a Christian household where he may fulfil his seasonal duties (748–62), Hautdesert appears as if in answer. The long and complex description which follows (763–806) is rooted in exact observation of contemporary castle architecture, but so conditioned by distance, perspective, and imagery as to create two conflicting effects: realism and fantasy (Davenport, pp. 149–50). Initially distant, elevated, but dwarfed by the forest about it; then *A castel þe comlokest þat euer knyȝt aȝte*, glimpsed by Gawain *As hit schemered and schon þurȝ þe schyre okez* of the tamed forest within the palisade of its park. The knight approaches until the castle towers above him, the moat unbridged, the gates shut, the outer wall *Of harde hewen ston*, deep rooted in the water, soaring up to the overhanging battlements; everything speaks of protection within (*Hit dut no wyndez blaste*) and resistance without (*A better barbican þat burne blusched vpon neuer*). Then, his rising glance, passing inward, is drawn amongst the turrets, chimneys, and carved pinnacles on the roof of the hall, a Gothic fantasy as insubstantial in its new-made, chalkwhite perfection as the paper castles which decorate the *soteltés* at a feast, *þat pared out of papure purely hit semed*. The final impression is of richness and beauty almost beyond belief in *a forest ful dep, þat ferly watz wylde*; a creation of man or of magic? black magic or white? – since beauty may bespeak good or disguise evil.[8]

Medieval readers might expect some guidance from tradition in a literary form which relied so heavily upon convention. But the tradition in this respect is as various as the wayside hospitality encountered by legions of knight-errants in two and a half centuries of romance: courteous reception in the house of a poor vavasour where, despite poverty of means, every delicacy of manner is displayed; equally courteous welcome by a hostess whose beds, however, are liable to be transfixed by flaming lances in the middle of the night; mystic experiences in a castle where grail and lance are carried in procession, but which next morning stands deserted.[9] The wayside castle has an obvious narrative convenience, since, in the characteristic *entrelacement* of romance, fresh adventures could arise there in the course of others, without causal explanation or long-term implications. There was always an element of the unexpected, often of the magical, in what happened there; they were as likely to be Douloureuse Garde as Joyeuse Garde; many were *chateaux de damoiselles* and sexual adventures were amongst the most frequent of their joys and perils; *lits périlleux*, of one kind and another, were common.

So Gawain lies, half asleep, in his gay bed at civilised Hautdesert, surrounded by a complex tradition which admits of many possibilities.

> And as in slomeryng he slode, sleȝly he herde
> A littel dyn at his dor, and dernly vpon   (1182–3)

What is he – what are we – to expect? *Hit watz þe ladi* . . . The Lady! – Bertilak's wife; we are not to know her by any other name and her marital status is at the core of her role in the poem. But what is her role to be? That of the romantic lady who, seduced by a knight's reputation, offers herself to him? Or the lady in distress who visits a guest in his bed seeking his help against her enemies? Or the seductive hostess who presses her sexual attentions on passing knight-errants? Or the wife of the Generous Host whose husband sends her to bed with guests, permitting kisses but nothing further? Or a medieval Potiphar's Wife who will avenge a repulse by making false accusations of rape? Or an agent of the Devil, a sexual snare for men's souls who, if firmly rebuffed, will vanish, taking her castle with her?[10] Romance tradition provides a wide variety of roles for ladies who steal into the bedroom of a visiting knight in the absence of their husbands (Burrow, pp. 80–1).

But the Lady of Hautdesert is already well known to us; does anything in what we know prepare us for her stealthy appearance in Gawain's bedroom? Everything we have previously seen of her at Hautdesert implies a chatelaine as noble, courteous, and welcoming as the lord. We meet her first on holy ground, and the immediate impression as she comes towards us through the chancel is of peerless beauty; *wener þen Wenore* she seems to Gawain (941–6). But suddenly, amongst the *mony cler burdez* who surround her, his eyes and ours light on her *alter ego* – ominously on her left, the antithesis of all her physical qualities, yet equally honoured by the castle company. The famous double portrait of the old lady and the young (947–69) has been exhaustively analysed elsewhere (Carson, pp. 5–9; Moon, pp. 39–46). Superficially it is immediately recognisable as a rhetorical device, the description by contrast (Pearsall, p. 131). But is the rhetoric intended to be functional or merely ornamental? And if functional, does it relate to character, to plot, or to moral theme? In allegorical literature, the rhetorical juxtaposing of youth and beauty in contrast with age and ugliness would imply opposition between them, between Good and Evil; but here the ladies go hand in hand! Some critics have seen them as one character under two aspects: Morgan le Fay, young and beautiful seductress of Arthur's knights, and *Morgain-la-déesse* (TGD, p. 129), enchantress withered by contact with evil forces in perverting the magic taught her by Merlin (Loomis, p. 89; Carson, p. 5; Moon, pp. 45–6). But though in retrospect their identity would have significant implications for the plot, is it sufficiently evident at this point to raise those implications? Equally, were firm identification of the elder lady as Morgan possible at this point, it would colour our whole view of Hautdesert, where she occupies that honourable place at table filled at Camelot by Bishop Baldwin, revealing her as the demonic centre of a false court (Gardner, p. 79). But our recognition of the enchantress and our judgement on the court must await the outcome of events.

Meanwhile, we are puzzled by the ambiguous use of rhetoric and by the detailed and vivid language in which its formulae are expressed, disturbed by the sensuous language (*fayrest in felle, of flesche and of lyre*; *Hir brest and hir bryȝt þrote bare displayed*; *lykkerwys on to lyk*) and sexual similies (*hillez* for 'breasts' in line 956 – Waldron, p. 71) applied to the younger lady, and repelled by the cruel terms, still sexual (*Hir buttokez balȝ and brode*) but grossly unfeminine (*ȝolȝe*; *Rugh ronkled chekez*; *blake chyn*; *blake broȝes*; *naked luppez*; *sellyly blered*) used of the elder – terms reminiscent of religious lyrics on the 'Signs of Old Age' or 'Signs of Death' (Waldron, p. 23). If the rhetorical effect is to raise allegorical echoes of human mortality, of the dwindling of Youth into Age, 'of the homiletic theme that age is a mirror of the frailty of the flesh' (Waldron, p. 23), the Lady's stealthy entry to Gawain's bedroom must raise moral as well as social expectations of a highly ambiguous kind. There have been sensual undertones to the society of Hautdesert even before the appearance of the ladies: the luxury of Gawain's bedroom (852–9), the glowing, spring-like colours, the rich stuffs and soft furs which replace his armour and renew his beauty (860–81), the warm fire before which he relaxes over wine and a profusion of delicately-prepared food (882–900). But it was spiritual rather than creature comforts which he had sought there (750–62); and, ironically, it is in the chapel that Mary's knight first sees the Lady, whose interest in him is immediate: *Þenne lyst þe lady to loke on þe knyȝt* (941). Despite the implication of physical interest in the verbs, there need be nothing more than social duty in her advancing to meet him, or due courtesy in his response:

> When Gawayn glyȝt on þat gay, þat graciously loked,
> Wyth leue laȝt of þe lorde he lent hem aȝaynes;
> Þe alder he haylses, heldande ful lowe,
> Þe loueloker he lappez a lyttel in armez,
> He kysses hir comlyly, and knyȝtly he melez.   (970–4)

Both forms of greeting are socially acceptable, but the distinction made between *Þe alder* and *Þe loueloker*, the distant bow, the intimate – but brief – embrace, and the sexual overtones of the kiss under the husband's eyes are inescapable. And the shifting syntax of the opening lines, where Gawain, with his eyes on the younger lady, advances to greet both, suggests a momentary confusion between the social forms – the lord's permission punctiliously requested – and dawning sexual interest. Whatever may have momentarily passed through Gawain's mind – or the Lady's! – the social forms provide a refuge for them all:

> Þay kallen hym of aquoyntaunce, and he hit quyk askez
> To be her seruaunt sothly, if hemself lyked.   (975–6)

Yet, even then, Gawain's discretion in seeking to be the courtly *seruaunt* of *both* the ladies is, perhaps, betrayed by the quickness with which he makes it and the nervousness of the syntax, *hit* belonging properly with *if hemself lyked* and *sothly* requiring some such verb as 'swears' rather than *askez*.

Thereafter, in the closed society of Hautdesert, at table in the great hall or with more intimate company over wine and talk and party games by the hearth in a private room, Gawain and the Lady are never alone – until she enters his bedroom on the morning after the other guests have taken their leave. Always there is the boisterous, unnoticing husband and the silent duenna-figure of honoured but unknown status in the background. Yet there is a sense of intimacy between them, of self-absorption to the exclusion of others:

> Bot ȝet I wot þat Wawen and þe wale burde
> Such comfort of her companynye caȝten togeder
> Þurȝ her dere dalyaunce of her derne wordez,
> Wyth clene cortays carp closed fro fylþe,
> Þat hor play watz passande vche prynce gomen,
>   in vayres.   (1010–15)

And their privy (*derne*) conversation in the company of others, its unstated subject, their pleasure in each other's society, words apart, the use of Courtly Love terms (*dalyaunce, cortays*), and terms which imply action as well as talk (*dalyaunce, play*), the association of their behaviour with the ambiguous, half-ominous *gomen*, even the very assertion of its innocence (*closed fro fylþe*) hints at something which unites them, sets them apart, something hidden, possibly amorous, potentially improper.

Between Gawain's first sight of the castle and the Lady's first entrance to his bedroom over four hundred lines have passed, apparently without significant action. In them the world of Hautdesert has been put before us, casually but intimately; far more intimately than Camelot, which is economically presented by evoking romance traditions and varying them significantly. Conventional romance patterns are also involved in establishing the court of Bertilak, but in such variety and so ambiguously that, without the established reputation of Arthur's court to reassure us, we have difficulty in deciding what our reactions and expectations should be: assurance born of Hautdesert's resemblance to the ideal world of Camelot, or anxiety that it may, like Camelot, prove less than ideal; confidence that it will conform in all respects to the benign rather than the malign variants of the traditions it evokes, or concern for the hero, disarmed by feasting, wine and festive sports and, apparently, susceptible to the social and sexual charms of the mistress of the castle. We may share his confidence that this substantial, civilised society is what it outwardly seems or feel, with some critics, 'that Gawain's crucial moral choice is to be made in a situation which is not quite "natural"' (Eadie, p. 302).[11]

If, without being able to define what is unnatural about it, we are puzzled or disturbed by the Lady's stealthy entrance to the hero's bedroom, we may expect to be guided by Gawain's reaction. It seems entirely human and instinctive: caution (1184–6); embarrassment, avoided by hasty recourse to feigned sleep (1189–90); outward composure covering emotional unease and social uncertainty (1195–9); resolved at length by an elaborate and self-conscious piece of play-acting, whose artifice is underlined by the ponderous syntax:

> Þen he wakenede, and wroth, and to hir warde torned,
> And vnlouked his yȝe-lyddez, and let as hym wondered,
> And sayned hym, as bi his saȝe þe sauer to worthe,
>   with hande.   (1200–3)

At which point, I think, we laugh; and, though we may not be able to define the cause of our laughter, it must materially affect our relationship to the hero hereafter.[12]

Our relationship to Gawain is largely conditioned by the way in which he has been presented up to this point, in a subtly changing sequence of roles, drawing heavily upon romance tradition but invoking it, as usual, ambiguously. He slips into the poem whose hero he is to be as one of a catalogue of Arthur's knights (109–15), sharing his dignity as the king's nephew with Agravain, but distinguished in the hierarchy by his seat of honour beside Guenever – which may also remind us of his frequent role as her protector and his general reputation as a 'squire of dames', the social relationship which he bears – initially – to Bertilak's lady. He is silent, like his companions, under the Green Knight's challenge and his scorn for the Round Table; ambiguously so, since we cannot tell which of the poet's qualifications – *not al for doute, / Bot sum for cortaysye* (246–7) – applies to him. But courtesy is the keynote of his intervention at the last moment, as Arthur is about to strike the blow which threatens eventual annihilation of the monarch (*þe kyng wyth croun*) and the kingdom (338–61). With punctilious politeness and a string of deferential conditional clauses, he expresses respect for the king and queen (343–7), distaste for the nature of the affair (but no open criticism of the folly of becoming involved in it) (348–50, 358) confidence in the courage of the stunned, silent court (351–3), self-abnegation coupled with pride of race (354–7), contempt for the challenge and half-confessed recognition of its potential danger (355, 358).

There is an element of contradiction in what he says – betrayed, perhaps, by some slight incoherence of syntax; but manner is more important here than matter, Gawain's courtly formality restoring the equilibrium of the Round Table in the face of the Green Knight's insults and the king's intemperance, giving his companions a hint to remember their reputation for valour, and providing an escape from the dilemma for king and court, without criticising them or vaunting his own foresight and courage. At the same time, the very formality of the speech establishes some keynotes in Gawain's characterisation: his social and verbal formulae; and the consequent difficulty of determining exactly what is in his mind on many occasions.[13] Here, for example, all his rationalising ends in an appeal to convention: that the contest should be his by right of first asking (359–61), an Arthurian usage as unquestioned and irrational as that which seemingly provoked the challenge, but requiring the judicial approval and involvement of the whole court. 'Gawain has tactfully imposed order and good sense on what had threatened to become chaos' (Donner, p. 310) – but what precisely is his own judgement of the situation?

The Green Knight catches his tone and the exchange between them is polite, formal, even legalistic in the statement of the terms of the Exchange of Blows compact (375–416). Gawain's attitude suggests that he has identified his opponent as the conventional knight-challenger of romance; but though he makes no open acknowledgement of the supernatural aspect of the apparition which had stunned the court, there are, perhaps, undertones of concern in his *'quat-so bifallez after'* and his stipulation that the return blow must be struck by the Green Knight in person (384–5). And though tact may be the appropriate response to a knight-challenger, it may equally be inadequate to deal with the wiles of a supernatural testing-agent who extracts Gawain's name without revealing his own, and ironically undermines Arthur's superficial confidence (372–4) by his ambiguous detachment in the face of what seems certain death (406–14). Since we cannot know the source of his confidence – chivalric courage or demonic pre-knowledge? – we are disturbed by the mixture of the coldblooded and the colloquially casual in his language. So also is Gawain, to judge from his flurry of unanswered questions (398–400).

But in action he is calm – *his ax he strokes* – and his beheading of the Green Knight is technically expert (415–26). His reaction to its astonishing outcome is ambiguous (427–86). He does not speak again in this fitt; a tactful silence in the face of an occurrence beyond chivalric experience, or an echo of the shocked and puzzled silence of the court? The court has at least recognised the occurrence as a *meruayl*, while Gawain's sole reaction associates him with Arthur, with whose earlier behaviour his own had been implicitly contrasted: *Þe kyng and Gawen þare / At þat grene þay laȝe and grenne* (463–4). If the king's laughter is unfeigned, it must confirm earlier impressions of the facile element in his personality;[14] if it is merely part of his dutiful effort to reassure the queen by equating the *selly* they have just seen with *laykyng of enterludes* and other Christmas *craft*, does Gawain sense any irony in the figurative meaning of his *'Heng vp þyn ax'* ('Have done with this business' – TGD, p. 87) or, accepting the literal meaning, does he see the axe on the wall as a memento of a *wonder* past and done with – as it is

implied others will do – or as a *memento mori* for the future?
If these ironies and ambiguities escape us as readers, the poet
draws our attention abruptly to what is or should be passing
through the hero's mind by ending the fitt with a direct
personal address to Gawain, silent amidst a renewal of the
rechles ('care-free' / 'careless') *merþes* (40) with which the
Camelot episode began:

> Now þenk wel, Sir Gawan,
> For woþe þat þou ne wonde
> Þis auenture for to frayn
> Þat þou hatz tan on honde.   (487–90)

Throughout the fitt, Gawain has been presented formally
rather than individually as an exemplar of knightly courtesy
and self-control, somewhat passively and negatively in contrast with and relation to others, and entirely externally,
without indication of his personal opinions. In Fitt II there is a
subtle mutation by which the private individual emerges from
the chivalric exemplar, and the reader is led from admiration
for the knight in shining armour to sympathy for the man
beneath it. The process is begun in the opening lines (491–9),
with their ambiguous comments on the significance of the
previous action and their sibylline hints as to its future outcome, their implication that Gawain, like his fellow knights,
had acted with the rash confidence that wine gives, and that,
like them and all men, he is susceptible to Fortune's ever-
turning wheel and the ceaseless cycles of time.[15] In particular,
these lines: *Gawan watz glad to begynne þose gomnez in halle*,
Bot þaʒ þe ende be heuy haf ʒe no wonder (495–6), by
implying an attitude on Gawain's part towards the earlier
events for which we have no objective evidence and affecting
to share with us some dark implication which would make
that attitude ill-advised, renew our curiousity as to his actual
view of events, sharpen our concern for him as the representative of chivalry in conflict with unknown forces, and at the
same time give us some sense of superiority and detachment
from him as a man of limited judgement and foresight. The
passage on the cycle of the seasons which follows (500–35),
with its insistence on growth and decay in nature, underscores
the theme of man's mortality; but does so by ironic counter-

point, since it is man's *absence* from the cycle of the seasons which reminds us that his fleshy mortality, not susceptible to cyclic renewal, makes the question of his spiritual immortality of particular importance (Silverstein, pp. 260–6; Tristram, pp. 111–12).

From the cycle of time we are brought back to a point in time, the Christian festival of Michaelmas, from nature to the court of Arthur, and from mankind in general to Sir Gawain: *Þen þenkkez Gawan ful sone / Of his anious uyage* (534–5). The verb reminds us of our last glimpse of Gawain in the previous fitt and of the poet's warning to him (487–90); the adjective (MED *anoious* adj., (*a*) 'troublesome, difficult; (*c*) grievous') ironically contrasts with the attitude attributed to him then; both renew our curiousity as to his real feelings. Now at least we learn what is in the mind of his fellow courtiers: superficially the Camelot of customary usages continues as before, *With much reuel and ryche,* but underneath:

> Al for luf of þat lede in longynge þay were,
> Bot neuer þe lece ne þe later þay neuened bot merþe:
> Mony ioylez for þat ientyle iapez þer maden.   (540–2)

Social hypocrisy or well-intentioned imitation of Gawain's courtly tact? His own tact seems somewhat strained by the strength of feeling underlying it:

> For after mete with mournyng he melez to his eme,
> And spekez of his passage, and pertly he sayde,
> 'Now, lege lorde of my lyf, leue I yow ask;
> 3e knowe þe cost of þis cace, kepe I no more
> To telle yow tenez þerof, neuer bot trifel'   (543–7)

Many commentators sense uneasy doubts behind his stiff upper lip (Pierle, pp. 208–9; Barron, pp. 9–10; Hunt (1976), p. 9), and the stoicism with which he faces his fate – '*Of destinés derf and dere / What may mon do bot fonde?*' (564–5) – acknowledges the danger of the mission as plainly as the more open fears of the court:

> Þat so worthé as Wawan schulde wende on þat ernde,
> To dry3e a delful dynt, and dele no more
>   wyth bronde.   (559–61)

There is a degree of verbal ambiguity in the expression of both which compels the reader to use his own judgement in weighing words and thoughts.[16] But the general contrast between the duplicity of the court and Gawain's stoical frankness is sufficient to win admiration for his courage and, at the same time, recognition of the natural fears over which it triumphs, allowing the reader to glimpse his common humanity in the hero.

In the arming scene which follows, humanity is cloaked in heroic conventions which present the type rather than the individual. The fundamental effect is reassuring for the reader: all heroes arm before adventures, so Gawain's arming attests his chivalric status, the splendour of his equipment asserts the glory of chivalry in general and his own in particular, while the symbolism inherent in the ceremony evokes the Christian basis of all knighthood. But there are elements not wholly consistent with the rhetorical function of the passage: the predominance of red and gold in the trappings of both man and horse, recalling the green and gold common to the Green Knight and his mount; an association between man and beast natural enough in that emenation of Nature, but symbolising what in Gawain's case? – the brute nature of the man beneath the armour? Then there is the disturbing congruity of colours itself – what common quality in Gawain and his opponent is symbolised by the gold? And there is the incongruity amidst all this panoply of war of the embroidered *vrysoun*, the handiwork of *mony burde*, with its reminder of Gawain's amorous reputation. Above all, there is the ironic uselessness of all this superb equipment against the undefended, presumably fatal, assault stipulated by the Exchange of Blows compact – implying, perhaps, the futility of heroism, the defencelessness of chivalry, in the face of certain foes.

The following description of the hero's shield and the itemisation of its device (619–65) assert the values of chivalry in a most confident and absolute form: rooted in Christian belief, aspiring to perfection in faith and works, expressed in a perfect figure, unending, unbroken, no line or point obscuring any other. It is a symbol of *trawþe* and, as a heraldic charge peculiar to Gawain, the badge of his aspiration to perfection in thought and deed, in faith in Christ the Redeemer and devotion to Mary the Intercessor, and in the practice of the chivalric virtues. The meaning of *trawþe* is complex, but its essential unity, the balanced interrelation of the qualities, mental, physical, spiritual, and social through which it is expressed, is emphatically implied in the perfect wholeness of the pentangle figure.[17] And yet there are features which seem to distort its symbolic significance: the shield, which bears on its outer surface the *nwe* pentangle, unfamiliar arms for Gawain, carries on its inner an ancient device, usually associated with Arthur (TGD, p. 95), an image of the Virgin, suggesting, perhaps, a special devotion to one of the five pentads; and amongst the elements of the fifth pentad there seems to be some discrimination in importance between the various virtues:

> . . . fraunchyse and fela3schyp *forbe al þyng*,
> His clannes and his cortaysye croked were neuer,
> And pité, *þat passez alle poyntez* . . .   (652–4)

– perhaps merely verbal, but suspicious in a context so painstakingly precise.

Apparently unconscious of any imbalance in his devotion to the chivalric code, Gawain prepares to depart: *And gef hem alle goud day,* / *He wende for euermore* (668–9). The blunt revelation of his inner thoughts recalls abruptly the half-hidden doubts of the previous scene, ironically undercutting the rhetorical convention and chivalric confidence of the arming interlude. Confirmation that Gawain, like his fellow knights, recognises the fatal nature of his mission, heightens the contrast between his stoical departure and their nervous whispering (670–90). The futility of their suggestion that the king should '*haf dy3t 3onder dere a duk to haue worþed*', their open recognition – after the event – of the challenger as '*an aluisch mon*', and their criticism of Arthur's '*angardez pryde*' in following a course of conduct which they themselves had advised, as they watch Gawain ride away in perspective, implies his moral as well as his physical isolation. The best of Camelot seems doomed to be '*britned to no3t*', and an excess of alliteration suggests the insincerity of the tears which are shed for him: *Wel much watz þe warme water þat waltered of y3en* (684).

The sparks which fly from his horse's heels (671), as at the Green Knight's departure (459), remind us that he too is bound for an unknown land (460–1). Isolation is the key-note of his journey (691–762):

> Hade he no fere bot his fole bi frythez and dounez,
> Ne no gome bot God bi gate wyth to karp   (695–6)

As he moves from the romance realm of Logres, through the familiar geography of North Wales and the Wirral, and back into the unknown regions beyond, he passes unscathed through the evils of a notorious haunt of outlaws, the familiar trials of knight-errantry and the bitterness of winter in the north-west. It is a knight-errantry which is made to seem unreal (Bercovitch, p. 32), its wayside adventures parodied in a breathless catalogue as the poet yields – no doubt consciously – to the facile alliteration and verbal haphazardness which characterise conventional alliterative poetry (720–2). But it is winter, rather than wayside *wodwos*, which proves the real adversary, testing Gawain, man and knight, exposing him to the forces of Nature like an animal, and reducing the panoply of arms to a comfortless icy carapace (729–32). In the wilderness of tangled trees, the knight is levelled with the brute creation whose suffering he shares (746–9). But though, like them, his body is subject to Nature, his concern is for his immortal soul and, conscious of his Christian duty, his prayer to Christ and Mary is for spiritual comfort in the Advent season. Are we intended to recognise Everyman beneath the armour; Everyman on his journey to keep an appointment with Death (Burrow, pp. 26–8), subject to loneliness and want, to the evils of the world around him and the harshness of Nature, by comparison with which the conventional trials of romance appear faintly ludicrous and the splendour of arms irrelevant (Davenport, pp. 182–3)? If so, we can equate his spiritual needs with our own and judge the sincerity of his impulse to prayer accordingly, noting that the Knight of the Pentangle, faultless in thought and deed, nevertheless *cryed for his mysdede*, invoking divine protection by the sign of the cross and the colloquial formula of all sinful humanity: '*Cros Kryst me spede!*' Shared physical experience and common spiritual need bring us close, for a moment, to the man beneath the armour.

But with his entrance into Hautdesert Gawain is enveloped again in chivalric formula and the atmosphere of romance. Everything in his reception there (807–59), the unusual politeness of the porter, the servants kneeling as he crosses the drawbridge, the procession of knights and squires who lead him to the hall, the welcoming words of his host, the splendour of the bedroom to which he is conducted, suggests that his quality and status have been recognised. But at his disarming in this other Camelot (860–83), the knight who emerges from the armour shows an aspect of his personality unknown in the formally correct, emotionally restrained figure at Arthur's court, sensuous youth and physical beauty:

> Þe ver by his uisage verayly hit semed
> Welneȝ to vche haþel, alle on hwes
> Lowande and lufly alle his lymmez vnder,
> Þat a comloker knyȝt neuer Kryst made
>   hem þoȝt.   (866–70)

There is nothing effeminate in the portrait, merely a shift of emphasis to the personal and physical graces of knighthood. Gawain is now seen (884–900) at ease before the fire, indulging in the feasting and merrymaking which had surrounded him at Camelot: *Þat mon much merþe con make, / For wyn in his hed þat wende* (899–900). His name once mentioned is instantly recognised in this courtly context, and his reputation known (901–27). But it is an ambiguous and mutable reputation, rooted in *prys and prowes and pured þewes* but ending in *luf-talkyng*. For the courtiers of Hautdesert, knightly deeds (*'sleȝtez of þewez'*) are associated with refined conversation (*'þe teccheles terms of talkyng noble'*), *nurture* with *speche*, and courtly conduct with courtly wooing:

> 'In menyng of manerez mere
> Þis burne now schal vus bryng
> I hope þat may hym here
> Schal lerne of luf-talkyng.'
>   (924–7)

It is a limited view of knighthood, but not an illegitimate one; a distortion of Gawain's pentangle, exalting the social virtues of the fifth pentad above the others and *felaȝschyp* and *cortaysye* above all,[18] but acknowledging an aspect of Gawain's reputation which the poet has already established by mentioning, amongst the hero's equipment, the *vrysoun* embroidered with symbols of love. However incongrous it may have seemed in that heroic context, the implication went unquestioned because the romances repeatedly associate Gawain with *mony burde* and never consistently with any one until, in the French tradition, he becomes the notorious philanderer of the Arthurian world, the skilled seducer who loves and leaves (Benson, pp. 104–5), progressively degraded by contrast with the passionate constancy of Lancelot, the spiritual constancy of Galahad (Whiting, p. 215). English romance-writers, who preferred him to all his Round Table companions, went on celebrating the old, uncomplicated, heart-free Gawain for his physical prowess and manly virtues until Malory introduced his amorous counterpart. Writing for a sophisticated audience aware of both traditions, the *Gawain*-poet evokes an interplay between them by juxtaposing them (Loomis (1963), p. 161; Benson, pp. 95–6). But he is also playing with disparate aspects of *cortaysye* itself, rooted in various refinements of the conduct appropriate to courts (Evans, p. 147): the protection and service which knighthood owes to weaker creatures, woman among them; the courteous speech and deference of manner due to ladies; the elegant wooing and verbal, if not physical, seduction to which such devotion leads (Spearing, pp. 199–201). Hautdesert's expectation of its guest encompasses both his reputations, narrowing ultimately to those amorous talents which seem most irrelevant to his present mission. And, to our surprise, there are signs, in his sensual awareness of the Lady at first meeting, in their growing intimacy thereafter, and their privy conversation even in the presence of her husband, that his old susceptibility makes him vulnerable to her – whatever she may portend.

If, therefore, knowing Gawain as intimately as we must by that stage of the poem and from so many perspectives of human association and literary tradition, we are moved to laugh at his reaction to the Lady's appearance in his bedroom, the source of our laughter must surely be highly ambivalent: amusement at a very natural human response to a situation

which might have provoked the same response from us; surprise that the pentangle knight, who has maintained his composure through all the dangers and stresses of the poem so far,
should panic in the face of such a domestic incident; embarrassment at the elaborate fiction he must act out to extricate
himself from a position instinctively adopted on the spur of
the moment; shock, perhaps, that he should use the sign of the
cross as part of his play-acting. The action of crossing himself
carries us back, by a favourite device of the *Gawain*-poet, to
its last occurrence at the end of the hero's prayer in the forest.
In the interim, our direct personal judgement of him has been
largely suspended, replaced within the walls of Hautdesert by
romantic presentation of courtly deportment, the judgement
of others, superficial and undifferentiated, on his reputation,
and vague glimpses of his amorous susceptibility. Our previous impression of Gawain as representative of our common
humanity, courageous under the trials of flesh and spirit,
conscious of sin but calling in sincerity upon his God is, by this
device, juxtaposed with his all too human counterpart, cowering in embarrassment beneath the bedclothes, acting a lie in
the face of an indefinable, seemingly trifling, threat, using a
sacred sign for purposes of deception. So our laughter at the
old Adam beneath the skin is undercut by recognising in him
the Christian Everyman with whom we had earlier associated
ourselves; it is the uneasy laughter of emotional uncertainty.[19]

That uncertainty is compounded by the many queries
raised by the implications of much that has passed in the
apparent stasis between the sign of the cross in the wood and
its repetition in the bedroom. The reader is constantly faced
with familiar romance situations, and repeatedly prevented
from accepting them at their conventional face-value by the
poem's ambiguous evocation of the complex tradition behind
them. He sees the hero hospitably received at a wayside castle
whose courtliness challenges comparison with Camelot; but is
Hautdesert in the tradition of Joyeuse Garde or Douloureuse
Garde (Davenport, p. 158)? Is its courtly usage a better guide
to its chivalric practice than Camelot's? Will its festive games
prove as ambivalent as those played there? He sees him
visited in his bed by the beautiful chatelaine; but to which
tradition of wayside hostesses does she belong? If she is

presented as a type of youth and beauty, what is her relation to the wrinkled beldame who is linked with her? Has what has passed between her and Gawain under her husband's eyes been merely social courtesy or dawning sexual interest? He sees Gawain, of whose complex reputation he has been reminded, in apparent panic at the first advances of a beautiful woman; can this be the aspirant to chivalric perfection cowering before the forces of evil, or the amorous knight unnerved by an unnatural reversal of the roles of pursuer and pursued? Or is it merely a subtle instance of Gawain's tact in avoiding social embarrassment? In answering these questions, the reader may find himself confused by emotional uncertainty as to where his sympathies lie: with the representative of his own higher aspirations, the Everyman for whom some new trial of the flesh seems imminent; or with the smiling Lady whose entrance has provoked in Gawain what seems a purely instinctive reaction such as he might despise in his own fallible humanity; with the timidity of the hunted, or the amusement of the huntress. And if he turns to the parallel hunting episode for guidance as to what his reaction should be, he finds the same emotional conflict: compassion for the driven deer, remembered pleasure in the lord's hunting.

In this condition of emotional confusion and thematic uncertainty, it might well occur to the reader to fall back upon romance convention for guidance and look for an emblematic or metaphorical relationship between the hunting and the bedroom episodes. The superficially conventional nature of the poem, its use, in the exposition of the pentangle, of a detailed symbolic itemisation reminiscent of didactic literature, and the frequency with which the hunt is allegorically interpreted in various types of contemporary text, might well point him in that direction. The wide variety of forms – Saint's Life, Epic, Romance, Lyric, Didactic Poem – in which the allegorised hunt figures in the literature of Western Europe from the thirteenth to the sixteenth centuries has recently been demonstrated by Marcelle Thiébaux.[20] Her study shows how the natural interest of contemporary society in hunting, particularly of stag and boar, as an aristocratic pursuit led to constant literary allusions, often rhetorically heightened and idealised, exploiting the ceremonial aspects of an increasingly ritualised pastime, and incorporating occasional images drawn from the iconography of the hunt evolved by exegetical authors of allegory, scriptural glosses, and bestiaries. The hunt of love, developed in Greek and Latin literature, occurs at least as early as Plato's *Sophist*, in which all human affairs are seen as subdivisions of a great pursuit, men preying upon one another through love as through war, tyranny, piracy, oratory, law, and conversation. Love's hunting, already used as simile or metaphor by the Greek playwrights, was developed in lyric poetry and prose: 'Whether the metaphorical pursuer is animal or human, the hunt's climax and denouement may be seen as adaptable by any moderately imaginative poet to an amatory purpose' (Thiébaux, p. 92). As in other forms of the symbolic hunt, the amorous hunter is often, inconspicuously or overtly, manipulated by an external force, a god whose power to drive him to love is ultimately traceable to Eros, the oldest, most powerful of the gods: 'later it may be Nature, Amours, Lady Venus or Frau Minne that delivers the blow to render him the impassioned quarry or drives him to his inescapable hunting' (p. 93). The fate of those who fail to acknowledge Love's power is shown in Ovid's *Metamorphoses* where men and women who resist normal sexual love are threatened with destruction or with loss of their humanity by being changed into beasts, birds, trees, flowers; often those who try to ignore their amorous pursuers by engaging in hunting become themselves victims of the chase.

The authority of Ovid persisted in medieval literature and the hunting imagery of his *Ars Amatoria* was widely imitated and developed. The *De arte honeste amandi* of Andreas Capellanus opens with an allusion to the whole matter of love in terms of a man's hunting; other, more obscure, writers developed the hunt to provide the narrative line in love allegories. In the mid thirteenth century *Li dis dou cerf amoreus*, the driven beast represents the woman whose thoughts and desires so harry her that Amours the hunter is finally able to bring her to her knees and force her, as the dying stag, to accept love. Conversely, Jean Acart de Hesdin writes of himself in *L'amoureuse prise* (1332) as driven by the beauties of the woman he loves, and by his own desires, until he lies at last mangled and begging for mercy. The flexibility of the hunt image as a means of expressing the complexities of sexual love is demonstrated by Hadamar von Laber's *Die Jagd* (mid fourteenth century) in which the hunter, the lamenting Minne servant, is determined never to make the kill, since consummation would be damaging to the beloved and demoralising to the man who desires her. Unfulfilled, their love turns the woman into a frivolous destroyer, her lover into her victim, expressing through the frustrated, inconclusive chase the conventionalised tensions familiar in Minnesang.

Medieval authors were equally inventive in their exploitation of other aspects of the hunt, whose narrative pattern of quest and conflict could be given various denouements: the hunter might be successful in killing the game, or be killed in its pursuit and so become himself a victim; or he might be doomed to an endless chase forever bound to his quarry. The quarry may represent an extension of his own nature, some restless, uncontrolled, or older aspect of himself by killing which he may achieve a moral victory and complete his passage to a new condition. On the other hand, the prize may not be the victim he originally set out to capture, but some other acquisition or burden of wisdom with which he must learn to endure. Equally, an unsuccessful struggle may result in the dissolution of his former identity; failing to survive the crisis to which the hunt has brought him, he is annihilated in the act.

In addition to the chase of love, Professor Thiébaux distinguishes three other principal types of experience traditionally expressed in literature in the form of a hunt. There is the sacred chase, in which the quarry is the emissary of a deity, benign or vengeful, sent to aid or punish the hunter – represented in medieval literature by Aelfric's Passion of St Eustace, where the stag who ordains the baptism of the virtuous Roman tribune is identified with Christ, and the familiar paradox of pursuer and victim exchanging roles as the converted saint grows more like the god is associated with the Christian concept of the victim victorious. There is the mortal chase, exemplified by Siegfried's death in the *Nibelungenlied*, where the hero's exchange of his role of hunter for that of victim is ironically foreshadowed in all the details of his hunting which, at the same time, exemplify his whole character and recall his earlier achievements. And there is the instructive chase, in which hunting guides the hero from a condition of ignorance to one of knowledge or self-knowledge – exemplified, according to Marcelle Thiébaux, by *Sir Gawain and the Green Knight* where one 'hunter', the Lady, snares the hero with the green lace, while Bertilak, who initially 'seems to be pursuing Gawain as the devil pursues men to ensnare them' (p. 80), ultimately brings him to knowledge of his faults.

I would suggest that the *Gawain*-poet's exploitation of the complex tradition of hunting as a literal, metaphorical, allegorical component of secular literature is much more subtle and complicated than this analysis implies, and that a sophisticated audience, familiar with the convention, would initially suspect here an instance of the hunt of love. The unexpectedness of the Lady's entry to her guest's bedroom, her stealthy closing of the door, the reminder of her beauty (*loflyest to beholde*), the impropriety of her seating herself on the bed within the curtain, the knowledge that by contemporary practice Gawain must be naked under the bedclothes, everything suggests a sexual approach (Spearing, p. 215). Gawain's own embarrassed reaction supports the impression that he has made the same judgement. While he lies doggo, we are left without guidance either from him or from the complex, contradictory romance traditions of wayside castles and their chatelaines: what are the implications of this approach, and what should be the proper chivalric response? The rhetorically trained reader whose mind turns to the simultaneous scene in the woods can only be disturbed by the potential parallel: while Bertilak, flushing the deer from their coverts, singles out the females and drives them before him in panic, shooting them down one by one in a cataclysm of noise, his Lady comes, with the click of a latch, stealing upon a single male, separated from his kind and lurking in comfort and security, and traps him naked in his bed by sitting gently down beside him. The congruity of pattern, implying that Gawain is to be hunted by the Lady, is underscored by the incongruity of detail, heightening the contrast between the brutal but natural activity in the wood and the seemingly innocent, inherently unnatural, inaction in the bedroom (Thiébaux, pp. 76–8). The poet has marked the intended contrast by emphasising:

> . . . þe fre lorde hade defende in fermysoun tyme
> Þat þer schulde no mon meue to þe male dere
>
> (1156–7)

by setting healthy clamour against the broken calm of slumber, and one set of confused emotions against another.[21] We are surely meant to reflect that though the harts *with þe hyȝe hedes* can go free there is no close season for knights (those who have *þe hyȝe hode* (2297)) whose chivalric reputation makes them fair game for evil forces which, tradition teaches, come in fair shapes as well as foul, female forms as well as male. The rhetorical implications are ominous, but the inversions of detail do not allow the outcome of the bedroom scene to be clearly foreseen in the fate of the deer. This uncertainty must itself be a source of tension underlying the episode, compounded by our ambivalent emotional attitude to both hunter and hunted in each case.

So if we laugh at Gawain's devious response to the Lady's approach, it must surely be uneasy laughter, undercut by concern for his compromising situation, by doubt as to how he himself judges it, as to whether his play-acting is inspired by tact or terror. By the hunting metaphor he is cast in the role of the deer and some critics have interpreted his behaviour as a reflection of their panic (Savage, pp. 40–4). I would suggest the poet intended that to be our response, initially, while we are still unsure that we have correctly identified the nature of the metaphorical hunt, or its implications for Gawain. But I agree with those who feel that the initial association with the deer is not sustained by Gawain's behaviour throughout the interview with the Lady (Burrow, p. 98; Spearing, p. 217; Gallant, p. 35). Confusion, flight, panic and 'death' is the pattern of behaviour prescribed for him by the hunting parallel; his actual behaviour is very different.

It is not the Lady who flushes him into the open; seeing himself trapped in his lair, he emerges of his own free will, for the sake of social appearances (*'More semly hit were . . .'*), in keeping with his traditional courtesy. Courtesy is to be his watchword (and his safeguard) throughout their interview (1208–1308). Verbal courtesy allows him to meet each of the Lady's advances on its own terms; resolutely ignoring the sexual implications of the language she uses, the courtly-love conceit of the *prisonnier d'amour*, while responding politely at the level of verbal convention; disguising his request for permission to rise and dress in a deferential cloak of conditional clauses; striving to maintain their relationship at its previous level of *clene cortays carp closed fro fylþe* (1013; cf. 1221); responding to the idiomatic rather than the literal sense of the formula in which she offers him her body, despite the other sexual innuendoes which surround it.[22] By his social tact and verbal skill, he maintains the reputation for *talkyng noble* and *luf-talkyng* with which the courtiers of Hautdesert credited him (910–27). The Lady, blurring the distinction between words and deeds, implying that the game of courtly love is merely a mask for sexual love, challenges his amorous reputation in terms of action, leading him to deny her interpretation with courteous ambiguity (*'I be not now he þat ȝe ofspeken'*)[23] and her to question his very identity (*'þat ȝe be Gawan, hit gotz in mynde'*). Within identity the issue of worth is also under question: the Lady praises Gawain's *honour* and *hendelayk*, his *prys* and *prowes*, ambiguous terms which she contrives to give sexual overtones and to equate with material wealth:

> 'Þe prys and þe prowes þat plesez al oþer,
> If I hit lakked oþer set at lyȝt, hit were littel daynté;
> Bot hit ar ladyes innoȝe þat leuer wer nowþe
> Haf þe, hende, in hor holde, as I þe habbe here,
> To daly with derely your daynté wordez,
> Keuer hem comfort and colen her carez,
> Þen much of þe garysoun oþer golde þat þay hauen.
> Bot I louue þat ilk lorde þat þe lyfte haldez,
> I haf hit holly in my honde þat al desyres,
>   þurȝe grace.'   (1249–58)

reducing Gawain to an object of desire to be bartered for and possessed (Mills, p. 618). He attempts to avoid the challenge in her compliments by declaring himself *wyȝe vnworþy* and reminding her that she is not free to *chepen and chose* since she has already chosen a better man:

'Iwysse, worþy,' quoþ þe wyȝe, 'ȝe haf waled wel better,
Bot I am proude of þe prys þat ȝe put on me,
And, soberly your seruaunt, my souerayn I holde yow,
And yowre knyȝt I becom, and Kryst yow forȝelde.'

(1276–9)

By insisting that he is her *seruaunt*, the relationship he freely
adopted towards *both* the Hautdesert ladies at first meeting
(976), Gawain reminds her of his status as her guest, finally
rejects her attempt (1240) to reverse the natural order of
courtly relationship, and re-establishes the proper relation of
self-devoted knight to sovereign lady, rather than helpless
captive to exigent mistress. They have reached deadlock; the
chivalric balance between dishonour and discourtesy has
been maintained:

And ay þe lady let lyk as hym loued mych;
Þe freke ferde with defence, and feted ful fayre

(1281–2)

The moral victory is Gawain's. The Lady snatches a token
victory at the last moment by claiming a kiss by right of
courtesy; but Gawain deprives it of the impropriety which the
bedroom setting might have given it by treating it as the
proper duty of a vassal and by supinely accepting rather than
giving it. Yet there is something slightly unnatural in the
Lady's momentary dominance here, as from time to time
throughout the scene, and equally something laughable in
Gawain's passivity in her arms contrasted with the evident
relief with which he springs out of bed on her departure. The
shifting balance between amusement and moral concern creates the tension; the former arising from the ambiguous significance given to conventional phrases and relationships by
the bedroom context, from the Lady's attempted reversal of
male and female roles, the sense of embarrassment underlying Gawain's efforts to maintain punctilious courtesy in an
awkward social and physical situation; the latter springing
from the unnaturalness of the Lady's initiative with its implication of seduction, heightened by the ambivalent tradition of
the welcoming chatelaine and the ominous implications of the
deer hunt. But the tension is gradually resolved, the hero is
not seduced, the Lady retires with only a trifling trophy,

Gawain gradually suppresses his initial instinctive reaction to emerge master of himself and of the situation.[24] He has not become the panic-stricken victim; the rhetorical function of the parallel hunt was apparently contrastive (McClure, p. 377). But, if so, was his huntress engaged merely in a social game without moral implications?

And if Gawain has been in no moral danger, what accounts for the sense of relief as he escapes from imprisonment in his bed, hurries to dress and goes *blyþely to masse* and then to his meal in an atmosphere of ordered Christian normality (1309–18)? By insisting on the participation of both ladies, *þe alder and þe ȝonge*, in their communal *solace*, the poet emphasises the sexual propriety of the situation. True, his blandness raises questions as to the complicity of the duenna in the wooing scene, but superficially we have been returned to the atmosphere of Christmas festivity in which Gawain *made myry al day, til þe mone rysed, / with game*. Logically, mood and sequence should continue to the resolution of that communal sport in the Exchange of Winnings.

Instead, we return abruptly, *bi þat þe sunne heldet*, to the lord and *his gamnez* in the wood. The hunt is effectively over, and the two stanzas which follow (1319–64) are concerned with the breaking of the deer, exactly and technically described. The technique and ceremonial involved were aristocratic interests of the age, part of the formalisation of feudal society and an extension of its passion for hunting, and, as such, figure prominently in the romances. But can their interest here be purely incidental, a display of hunting science for knowledgeable readers? If the equally technical driving of the deer is thought to have a metaphorical significance related to the intercalated wooing scene, should that interrelationship not subsist in the pendant so carefully time-connected? If so, what bearing could it have on the hunt of love?

Hunting ends in death; if the Lady is pursuing Gawain, will that hunt also end in death? If so, what form of death is pre-figured in the metaphor of the breaking of the deer? A death involving disembowelling (1330–52), beheading (1353), and the division of the body into parts (1354–7). This suggests to me the disembowelling, beheading, and quartering which was the distinctive form of execution reserved for traitors in the Middle Ages. I hope to show that there are presumptive grounds for a charge of petty treason against Gawain in the kiss pressed upon him by the Lady, which, by the Exchange of Winnings compact, must be passed on to her husband on his return from the hunt. Readers aware of the complex tradition of the Generous Host must inevitably wonder whether his response to the kiss will conform to the violent or the benign version of the role. Those familiar with the various exploitations of the chase in secular literature might accept that the metaphorical hunt should end in the death of the quarry. Even readers with conventional expectations, disorientated by the cumulative effect of intermixed convention and innovation, by the conflicting demands made upon their emotions, and by the disturbing atmosphere of mingled concern and amusement, laughter and tension in bedroom and hunting field, might – momentarily at least – entertain the possibility that Gawain was to die a traitor's death at the hands of Bertilak.[25] But I doubt if, at this stage in the poem, they would entertain the idea for long – or were seriously intended to do so.

For with the return of Bertilak there is no renewal of tension: *When Gawayn wyth hym mette / Þer watz bot wele at wylle* (1370–1). This mood persists through the exchange of venison for the kiss, the supper and fireside chat, and the renewal of the Exchange of Winnings compact which follows (1372–1411). The reader may notice that there is much word-play on the comparative values of the goods exchanged, some rather pointed jocularity on the source of the kiss, and the same quasi-legal ceremonial as before in the renewing of the compact, but the slightly uneasy undertone created may not seem significant at a first reading. Later, however, when the second hunt ends in a ceremonial unlacing of the boar which bears an even closer resemblance to the traditional penalty for treason, he may begin to have second thoughts. And when, on the third day, the fox is stripped of his skin with unceremonious brutality, the variation within the repeated pattern may suggest a rare but notorious alternative to the traditional penalty – flaying alive!

NOTES

1   The interrelations of these ambiguities of structure, rhetoric, symbolism, and atmosphere are complex and difficult to state briefly; I have attempted it more fully elsewhere (Barron (1973), pp. 13–22). Other recent publications show that there is an increasing awareness of the deliberate and functional use of ambiguity in the poem (Eadie, p. 304, n. 19; Goldhurst, p. 61; Taylor, p. 1), and the ironic treatment of familiar conventions: 'a notable consequence being the difficulty which we experience in evaluating *in the context of the poem* motifs which we easily recognise as the common property of the romance genre. The texture of the poem, both semantically and ethically, is far from transparent. The *Gawain*-poet is essentially a critical rather than a didactic writer and his account of the hero's adventures challenges the reader's powers of discrimination at every stage' (Hunt (1976), p. 1).

2   Having established this relationship meticulously on the first day, he is less precise on the other two, though with the same general intention. Textual citations and references throughout are to the TGD edition.

3   See the various notes on the passage in TGD, pp. 105–8 and 110–13.

4   J. D. Burnley (p. 4) finds both aspects of the hunt equally unemotive, but T. Hunt ((1976), p. 12) detects an ominous note in the opening lines.

5   I interpret this passage (p. 169) as referring to a game of forfeits played between the sexes, in which small tokens concealed in the hand (*hondselle*) are awarded to ladies who correctly guess their nature or which hand contains them, while those who fail pay the forfeit of a kiss; 'as such it is the first in a series of games played for higher stakes, where what may be lost is one's head or one's honour' (Wilson, pp. 118–19).

6   Since so much in the behaviour of Arthur and his followers is left to the reader's own judgement, opinions invariably differ as to how far Camelot's reputation is compromised by the events of Fitt I. But the opening lines of Fitt II (491–9), themselves highly ambiguous, seem to imply that Arthur, who had longed for a tale of *sum auenturus þyng* (93), has received an actual *auenture* (250; OED *adventure* n., 5 'prodigy, marvel') instead; that it may prove a token of good or ill luck in the new year (*cf.* MED *hanselle* n., 1(*a*) and (*b*)) as ambivalent as the forfeits in the kissing game amongst his courtiers (see above, n. 5); that the challenge (*ȝelpyng*) he longed for may actually have been invoked by his court's pride in its chivalric reputation (OED *yelping* n., 1 'boasting, proud or pompous talk'); that the empty chatter of the feast (or the stunned silence which followed the challenge) is now to be replaced by serious business involving the Green Knight's axe (*stafful*, 'as full as one's hand is when holding a staff', Waldron, p. 52); that what began happily as a game may end sadly in earnest; that though, like many human concerns, it may have been undertaken light-heartedly under the influence of drink, man is susceptible to the changes of time and fortune and, though the cycle of the year may be endlessly repeated, his life is linear and finite. Benson (p. 100) comments:

'That other Camelot, the flawed Camelot of tradition, hovers always in the background and lends ironic depth to this Camelot, the idealised seat of courtesy.'

7   Perhaps to stimulate the reader to appreciate the various possibilities in the congruity between Camelot and Hautdesert, the poet has made particularly ambiguous use of the games at both. Bertilak's challenge to a contest of mirth-making for the possession of his hood set up on a spear (981–7) has the form of a popular village sport; but might it not also recall the tourneys and jousts (41–3) so lightly included amongst the other *caroles* (OED *carol* n., 1(*b*) 'diversions or merry-making') of Arthur's Christmas festivities? If both forms of mimic combat are appropriate to the season, it would be as ill-bred of Gawain to reject the Exchange of Winnings compact as to cavil at the contest over the forfeits at Camelot. If I am right (see above, n. 5) in thinking that the forfeits include both token gifts and kisses, the involvement of both in the Exchange of Winnings may initially make it seem more innocent, but ultimately more ominous when it involves the issues of the ownership of a gift – the girdle – which is also a token of ambivalent value. Equally, the contest for the hood may seem retrospectively more significant when the girdle becomes involved in Gawain's shifts to save his head in the Exchange of Blows and his opponent begins to pun upon *hode* (*MED hod* n., 2(*b*) 'the hood worn by . . . knights of chivalric orders' and MED *hode* n., 1(*a*) 'the order of knighthood' – as conferred on Gawain by Arthur (2297–8)).

8   Pearsall (p. 133) sees the concrete detail as subservient to a rhetorical end, the 'praise' of the castle in the *laus urbis* tradition; but is the rhetoric to be taken at its face value or undercut by the emotion roused by the disparate detail, its atmospheric associations, and the manner and sequence of its presentation? Waldron (pp. 8–9) notes that the reader shares Gawain's angle of vision and his emotional attitude: 'We are also aware of the wall as a barrier and can detect something of the mood which directs and colours his perceptions, the sense of isolation bred in a man by weeks of privation and loneliness.'

9   The references are all to romances of Chrétien de Troyes, respectively *Erec et Enide* (ed. M. Roques, CFMA, Paris, 1968), ll. 342–746, *Le Chevalier de la Charrete* (ed. M. Roques, CFMA, Paris, 1969), ll. 395–534, and *Le Roman de Perceval* (ed. W. Roach, Paris, 1959), ll. 3035–421.

10   These few examples of a recurrent romance situation are drawn respectively from: the Brun de Branlant episode of the First Continuation of Chrétien's *Perceval* (vol. I, ed. W. Roach, Philadelphia, 1949), ll. 2546–723; the Blancheflor episode of Chrétien's *Perceval*, *edn. cit.*, ll. 1699–2975; Chrétien's *Chevalier de la Charrete*, *edn. cit.*, ll. 1184–280; *Syre Gawene and the Carle of Carelyle* (ed. A. Kurvinen, Helsinki, 1951), ll. 445–68; the Potiphar's Wife motif occurs in a number of romances, including *The Seven Sages of Rome*, *Guingamor*, *La Chastelaine de Vergi*, *Lanval* and its various English derivatives; Malory's *Sir Bors* (*Le Morte Darthur*, bk. XVI) is one of many knights to encounter seductive ladies who are agents of the Devil.

11   'The much praised "realism" of these central scenes is a realism of detail, not a realism of overall situation. It is a device to draw the audience more and more into the private world of Gawain's testing so that the audience experiences with Gawain the anguish and suffering that he experiences, and they accept with Gawain the improbabilities that he accepts' (Eadie, p. 302).

12   'All this is pure comedy, the comedy of embarrassment . . .; and it sets the tone for the first part of the conversation which ensues' (Burrow, p. 78); 'We might momentarily have been inclined to smile at Gawain's mechanically hiding under the covers, pretending to sleep, but are inhibited by the fact that the diction used by the poet to describe the Lady's entrance makes us apprehensive and that the events are unfolded from Gawain's point of view' (Butturff, p. 143).

13   'No matter what the situation, no matter who the person, Gawain instinctively adopts the tone and manner best suited to the occasion' (Donner, p. 307).

14   Since *grenne* (MED *grennen* v., 1(*a*) 'to bare the teeth, grimace; also, snarl or growl'; 3(*a*) 'to sneer, scoff, laugh unpleasantly') had no humorous senses at this period, its ambiguous association with *la3e* can only suggest uneasy undertones in the reaction of Arthur and Gawain. 'Thus the episode comes to an end which is no end, with gaiety that is no gaiety. Our hero is in trouble and we know it' (Silverstein, p. 259).

15   See above, n. 6.

16   The court's *and dele no more wyth bronde* may mean 'and strike no blow in return' or 'and never strike another blow' (Waldron, p. 55); equally when Gawain speaks *with mournyng* he may be expressing not 'regret, sorrow' (TGD, p. 200) but rather 'concern' (Barron, p. 57).

17   'Just as a broken pentangle loses its magical power, so "truth" loses its moral power if it is "sundered" in any of its parts; for it is an ideal of *integrity* or oneness' (Burrow, p. 50). 'As the pentangle may be drawn in one continuous movement, so it becomes the symbol of the complete man, whose integrity admits no imperfection' (Engelhardt, p. 218).

18   'Where the author tells us that Gawain was morally spotless and *wyth vertuez ennoured* (634), that he *watz for gode knawen, and as golde pured* (633), the courtiers appear to see his *pured þewes* (912) simply in terms of social refinement, of a courtesy which was but one of the virtues of the pentangle' (Wilson, p. 122).

19   'From the moment his hostess Lady Bertilak steps into Gawain's bed-chamber we are permitted the happily imperfect view of him, his embarrassments, pretences, hesitations, doubts, and eventually his *wallande joye*, in short, his entire quandry as a man in an awkward moral and social situation, needing to make a decorous choice and ingeniously temporizing. With the unlocking of his eyelids, we gain the equivocal inner perspective which will continue on to the scene at the Green Chapel where the hero looks down at the drops of his own blood in the snow. Self-consciousness and the interior vision begun in the bed-chamber culminate, . . . in the hero's discovery and acknowledgement of human failings' (Thiébaux, p. 73).

20   Marcelle Thiébaux, *The Stag of Love: The Chase in Medieval Litera-ture*, Ithaca, N.Y., 1974.

21   The sound contrast, and the contrast of atmosphere to which it contributes, seem to me symptomatic of the poet's method here. For some critics it is precisely this contrast which rules out any possibility of a symbolic parallel between the hunting and the wooing (TGD, p. 107), but an inverted parallel can be as potent as a direct one, particularly in the context of the metaphorical hunt where the roles of pursuer and pursued are often reversed. For further examples of sound contrast as a means of thematic emphasis see Renoir, pp. 14–30.

22   Though there is now general agreement that *ȝe ar welcum to my cors* (1237) can be read innocently, D. Mills (pp. 615–16) suggests word-plays with sexual connotations on *tale* (1236; representing both O.E. *talu*, 'talk' and O.E. *tægl*, 'tail'), on *won* (1238; 'delight', but also 'dwelling'), and on *cors* itself (*cors*, 'body' and *cor(t)s*, 'courts'), which must have made it difficult for the original audience to ignore the less innocent implications of the whole.

23   Burrow (p. 83) suggests that Gawain implies both '*I* am not that' and 'I am not *that*', demonstrating 'both his courtesy and (covertly) his aware-ness that courtesy is not everything'. The *now* seems to me equally ambigu-ous, implying 'I am not the amorous knight under these circumstances, with my host's wife', or 'while on such a fatal mission' – one of many indications that the Green Chapel is never far from Gawain's mind at Hautdesert.

24   The poet has, I think, supplied indications of Gawain's gradual recovery of his self-possession in the epithets applied to him: in his first response to the Lady's attack, he is *Gawayn þe blyþe* (1213), and the ironic unsuitability of its application to the *schamed* knight is underlined by its bearing the lexically free, non-alliterating stress of the line; equally one may doubt the sincerity of his *mony a blyþe laȝter* (1217) a few lines later; mid-way in the interview he may be more at ease, but *þe myry mon* (1263) seems too emphatic for one who is still responding to the Lady's *gret chere* with *speches skere*; right to the end he behaves with constraint (*defence*, 1282), agreeing to her withdrawal with suspicious alacrity (1289); only as he goes out *blyþely to masse* (1311) can one sense that his feelings are being described without irony.

25   'The play upon the word *gomen* (*game*) (see, e.g., 1314, 1319, 1532, 1536, 1894) links the boudoir battle of wits with the slaughter in the field and hints that the sort of *gomen* enjoyed by Gawain and the lady may possibly have bloody consequences too' (Waldron, p. 22). 'It becomes very clear at Hautdesert that Gawain prizes his ability in a ritualised version of love which – as far as he is concerned – exists completely independently of the reality the games imitate; what the Lady tries to do is to convert the imitations into the corresponding reality and, ultimately, into death, for one cannot but feel retrospectively that Gawain's life is at stake in these scenes' (Hughes, p. 224).

II *TRAWTHE* AND TREASON

Students of romance are becoming increasingly aware of the important role played by law in the lives of the feudal noblemen for whom such literature was originally produced, men whose ruling function required them not only to administer justice but to interpret and even make the law. We have recently been reminded of the natural interrelationship of romance literature and vernacular codes, both derived from oral tradition, both publicly affirming and preserving the ideals and values of the ruling class: 'There are few sustained narrative works belonging to the twelfth and thirteenth centuries that do not contain a trial'; '. . . the inclusion of at least one scene of judicial combat, oath, or ordeal appears to have been a *sine qua non* of poetic production'.[1] Treason as a felony, a fundamental breach of the feudal bond between lord and man, figures largely in romance as the characteristic crime of chivalric society.[2] As the Middle Ages advanced, many distinct forms were defined in terms of the various aspects of that bond, always involving some betrayal of trust, whether formulated socially in terms of friendship or, later, technically in terms of fealty (Barron (1978), pp. 53–5).[3] In England, *The Great Statute of Treasons* of 1352 distinguished high treason as any crime against the king's person and regality – compassing or plotting his death, or that of his heir, violating his wife or daughters, etc. – from the petty variety involving similar offences against a lesser liege.

The codes express condemnation of these and other forms of treason which struck at the roots of social order – counterfeiting the ruler's coinage, falsifying his seal, spreading heresy, practising sorcery – in moral as well as legal terms. The moral failing inherent in his breach of troth put the traitor beyond the reach of mercy or compassion: 'He should perish in torments to which hell-fire will seem a relief.'[4] The form of execution might vary at the whim of the sovereign or judge, with local usage, or the sex of the victim – women being burnt alive to avoid the indecent exposure of their bodies in public (Barron (1978), pp. 56–7 and 59–60). The multiple penalties involved in many cases – dragging at the horse's tail, hanging, emasculation, disembowelling, beheading, quartering – show an obvious intention to humiliate the victim by subjecting him to a prolonged, painful, and ignoble death in public, to provide a warning to others by exposing his dismembered body in various parts of the realm, and to underscore the moral basis of his punishment by giving symbolic significance to its various elements.[5]

Though flaying alive undoubtedly figured amongst the penalties for treason, it can only have been a rare, and in England possibly irregular, variant of the customary punishment. Some Anglo-Saxon codes prescribe scalping for repeated law-breaking and a passage (possibly corrupt) in the *Leges Henrici Primi*, giving scalping or flaying as the penalty for the murder of a feudal superior, may reflect confusion on the part of post-Conquest compilers between a traditional native penalty and its continental counterpart (Barron (1978) pp. 56–7). At least one of the written statutes of France, the comparatively late record of earlier oral and regional codes, lists flaying amongst other barbaric penalties for treason.[6] And French history records a number of instances in which it was actually inflicted: under formal legal circumstances, for betraying a lord's castle to his enemies, for spiritual treason by plotting the death of a pope by sorcery, for sexual treason by adultery with women of the royal family; and irregularly as an act of mob violence against nobles judged to have betrayed a political or religious cause (Barron (1978), pp. 60–1).[7] That popular feeling in England as in France felt that flaying was a fit death for traitors is, perhaps, reflected in a variant version of the death of Richard Coeur-de-lion, fatally wounded by a common soldier while besieging one of his own rebellious vassals – technically an act of treason for which his killer is said in some unreliable chronicles to have been flayed alive (Barron (1978), p. 62). Of the other recorded instances in English history known to me, one was an act of contempt committed on the dead body of a tyrannical lieutenant of Edward I in the course of his Scottish wars, the other a sentence awarded by a kangaroo court amongst the retinue of a prince who had accused one of their number of treason, but never carried out (Barron (1978), pp. 57–8).

Whether or not the legal and historical records have still more instances to yield, flaying occurs in the literature of both France and England with greater frequency than the factual references would seem to warrant; and in both there is the same persistent association with various forms of treason. In the English romances, so often based on French originals, flaying alive is the characteristic death inflicted on Christian knights captured by giants, pagans, Saracens – an indication of the inherent barbarity of their traditional foes; paradoxically, it is also the death thought appropriate to giants, pagans, Saracens whenever they fall into the hands of Christian knights – appropriate because they have rebelled against God or know nothing of him. In both it is the ultimate threat of tyrants and other men of violence: in Laȝamon's *Brut*, the Emperor Lucius threatens to flay Arthur's soldiers, as vassals of one whom he considers a rebellious vassal; in *Guy of Warwick*, the Emperor of Germany makes the same threat against the defenders of a city in revolt; the tyrant Astriages flays St Bartholomew for converting many of his people, and pilgrims on their way to Jerusalem are martyred by the same method. Most of the various types of treason are punished in this way: the sexual treason of a knight who seduced the daughter of an emperor; the spiritual treason of Julian the Apostate, flayed after death by order of the Persian king Sapor and his skin nailed to the palace door, and of Caiaphas and those complicit with him in the crucifixion of Christ, flayed alive by order of Vespasian; the judical treason of a royal officer in the story of a venal Persian judge whose flayed skin is used to cover the judicial bench on which his son and successor must preside; high treason in the punishment suggested by Arthur's court for their fellow-knights who, in Chrétien's *Cligés*, fight for the rebel Angrès, Count of Guinesores, against the king; he, mercifully, merely has them dragged at the horse's tail under the walls of Windsor and the eyes of their fellow rebels.[8]

French authors appear to have made most creative use of flaying as a thematic motif. As one of the penalties which threaten those who, like the hero of Chrétien's *Lancelot*, have to ride in the shameful cart, it may be an ironic reminder that Lancelot, in passionate pursuit of the mission to rescue his lord's wife, was also on his way to commit sexual treason with her. In *Le Roman du Comte d'Anjou* by Jehan Maillart, a notary and officer of the chancellery under Philippe-le-Bel, it is the death decreed by the count's seigniorial court upon his aunt for having counterfeited letters from her nephew and feudal superior. She is sentenced to be flayed limb by limb, day by day, then salted and dropped into a privy. By the count's mercy, she is instead burnt alive. That such punishments could be thought appropriate to a noblewoman in a romance whose legal exactitude reflects the profession of its author, suggests the serious view taken of that form of treason which, by falsifying the coin or seal or sign manual of the lord, undermined the economic or legal basis of his authority. There is a similar threat to the legitimacy of the royal succession in the 'False Guinevere' episode of the *Prose Lancelot*, part of the Vulgate Cycle, when Arthur is falsely persuaded that Guinevere is not his true queen but an imposter substituted for her on the wedding night. He unwisely submits the matter to the judgement of the baronial court of the Lady of Carmelide who claims to be the real queen; it sentences Guinevere, as a penalty symbolic of the form of her supposed treason, to be flayed on the head which had wrongly received the crown and the palms of the hands anointed with the coronation oils. When the False Guinevere, stricken with paralysis by divine retribution, confesses her lying accusation, she is condemned to the same penalty in accordance with the contemporary legal principle that the false accuser should suffer the pains to which he had exposed another.[9]

The only fully-developed instance of flaying in a Middle English romance known to me, in the thirteenth-century *Havelok the Dane*, is less subtle thematically but technically exact in its knowledge of the social and legal significance of the penalty. The plot contains two parallel examples of treason, the guardians of both the princely hero and the heroine betraying the trust placed in them by plotting against their wards. The boy, Havelok, having recovered both patrimonies, brings the traitors to justice. Godrich is simply burnt alive, perhaps because his victim was merely feminine. But Earl Godard, the trusted friend of Havelok's father, *þe fule swike* whose treason is compared with that of Judas, is condemned by the judgement of his peers to be flayed alive and then drawn to the gallows at a mare's tail. The order of the penalties is paralleled in history; the details of the drawing over the fallows behind a female beast, scabbed and broken down, have the malicious exactitude of folktale. The flaying is described in minute and pitiless detail, without horror or compassion; *Daþeit hwo recke! he was fals* – the judgement which justifies the utmost cruelty towards a noble who has behaved like a villein, a vassal who has become a felon.[10]

In what little we know of the punishment of treason in medieval life and literature certain features seem to me particularly relevant to *Sir Gawain*: the persistent association of the twin forms of the felony, high treason and petty treason, as resting on the same moral basis of breach of trust; the definition of that trust in terms of friendship rather than as a formal feudal contract; the underlying implication that treason, as a felony, involved moral delinquency as well as social deviance and was deserving of hatred and contempt; the marking of society's abhorrence of treachery by two particularly cruel and degrading forms of execution, both involving elements of symbolic significance; the strong impression made upon the contemporary imagination by the rare instances of flaying for this crime, and its particular fascination for the writers of chivalric romance. I believe that allusion is made to both forms of execution in the third fitt of *Sir Gawain*. If so, how are those allusions made operative in the scheme of the poem and what are their implications for its theme?

I would suggest that, like many other elements in the tripartite structure of Fitt III, the effect of the interrelation of the hunting and the wooing cannot be fully appreciated at a first reading. Since the overall pattern of the fitt is variation within repetition, each element gains in meaning and force by being repeated and the cumulative effect is given new significance by the final variation. In many cases, the thematic contribution will not become clear until the fourth fitt and then only through the reader's perception of the overall design, without being made openly explicit. Any critical commentary which is precise as to when and how a particular element will become operative, and what it will contribute to the thematic outcome, courts error by generalising upon effects designed for individual sensibilities of varying degrees of perception. With that risk in mind, I would suggest that readers whose familiarity with the hunt of love led them to suspect that Bertilak's hunting of the deer had a metaphorical bearing upon the Lady's wooing of Gawain might logically expect that relationship to extend to the outcome of the hunt in the death and breaking of the deer. By a literal application of the parallel, Gawain should die at the Lady's hands; a barely tenable eventuality which evaporates in the relaxed mood at the end of the bedroom scene, suggesting the possibility that the rhetorical connection between hunting and wooing may be by inversion in outcome as well as in incidental detail, the hunt of female by male ending in a holocaust, while the female hunting the male sees her quarry escape. The unexpected return to the hunting field, with its insistence on the importance of Bertilak's activities in the strict economy of the poem, revives the suspicion that they have some bearing on his wife's wooing of Gawain. The ceremonial butchery there postpones the expected pendant to the bedroom scene, the surrender of the kiss to the husband. If any anxiety as to what construction he will put upon such a trophy crosses the reader's mind, it may well be increased by other considerations: a kiss is so often the symbol of greater sexual favours; by tradition the Generous Host may permit the one but prohibit and punish the other; the Lady, by pressing her attentions upon Gawain, suggests a role for her husband more ominous than his previous presentation had implied.

Bertilak is first presented in the context of his court, at the climax of Gawain's ceremonious induction there (807–41); our initial reaction to him is likely to be conditioned by the ambivalent tradition of wayside castles in romance, by the miraculous appearance of so sophisticated a dwelling in such a barbaric setting, and by the conflicting impressions of reality and fantasy suggested by its descriptions (see above, pp. 6–8). But in the overall presentation of Hautdesert, the predominant impression is its resemblance to Camelot as a place of courteous welcome, ordered ceremony, religious observance, and seasonal festivity, and in such a setting Bertilak appears, in Gawain's eyes, another Arthur, a man fit *To lede a lortschyp in lee of leudez ful gode* (849). His physical description is that of a proper man, as solidly substantial as – in one aspect – his castle seems:

> A hoge haþel for þe nonez, and of hyghe eldee;
> Brode, bryȝt, watz his berde, and al beuer-hwed,
> Sturne, stif on þe stryþþe on stalworth schonkez,
> Felle face as þe fyre, and fre of hys speche;   (844–7)

But if there are parallels to the kingly bearing of Arthur in his upright stance, bold face, and easy nobility of speech (*cf.* 103–8), there are also disturbing echoes of the Green Knight in his huge size (*cf.* 137–41), unfashionably full beard (*cf.* 180–6), and the animal associations suggested by its colour.[11] There is much laughter at his court as at Camelot, but his own laughter suggests at times the ironic mockery of the Green Knight (908–9, 1068; *cf.* 316, 2389), at others the innocent merriment of Christmas festivity (988–990).[12] There is every sign of respect and courtesy in his treatment of his guest, yet, like the Green Knight, he learns Gawain's name without revealing his own (901–9; *cf.* 379–89, 398–411, 448–55) – an ominous circumstance in romance and folktale.[13] Christmas is celebrated in his court, as at Camelot, with the religious ceremonies (930–2; *cf.* 62–5) and secular sports (981–7; *cf.* 41–9, 66–70) proper to the season; what distinguishes Bertilak is the violent energy with which he keeps up the celebrations:

> Þe lorde luflych aloft lepez ful ofte,
> Mynned merthe to be made vpon mony syþez,   (981–2)

His eagerness may echo the boyish restlessness of Arthur (85–9) (Burrow, p. 65), and carry the same implication that such impulsive behaviour is inappropriate in the leader of a courtly society, or it may remind us of the controlled violence of the Green Knight (136, 199–202, 221–2, 303–8, 329, 430–43, 457–9), suggestive of a force of nature (Benson, pp. 93–4). This, and other characteristics which link Bertilak and the Green Knight, have been interpreted as demonic (McAlindon, pp. 330–1), but what in the one seems uncouth and threatening is no more than mildly uncourtly and comic in the other (Benson, pp. 87–9). I would suggest that the links with Arthur, though less obvious, are no less significant.[14] Together they present Bertilak as an ambivalent figure, superficially the courteous, good-natured, ebullient lord of a sophisticated society, but with an excess of animal spirits which raises disturbing echoes of an earlier amalgam of the courtly and the uncouth in whom the imbalance of nature and nurture proved ominous. At a first reading, before his association with the Green Knight is known, the reader has no alternative but to accept Bertilak as what he professes to be, since the poet offers no guidance in discriminating between his benevolent role as host and the ominous undertones in his characterisation.[15]

Any uneasiness the reader may feel is, however, compounded by the ambiguity inherent in the role of host in medieval romance. The tradition allows for a variety of interpretations in relation to the requirements of formulaic plots: if the hero is to be sheltered until his wounds heal, he will find refuge in a castle whose lord shares his own chivalric values; if he is to be tested, he may find himself in the stronghold of some Black Knight whose hatred of chivalry expresses itself in the perversion of its obligations of hospitality and fair dealing. Everything in Bertilak's overt behaviour towards Gawain identifies him as the Generous Host; Gawain's punctilious but easy response shows that he recognises him as such and knows his own obligations towards him:

He has, in Malory's phrase, Bercilak's meat and drink in his body; and one function of the poet's scenes of dining, supping and drinking is to establish this fact in the reader's imagination – host and guest becoming 'fellows' as they feast together over Christmas. The sense of this fellowship runs right through the two central fitts of the poem. The exchange of winnings, for example, is, from this point of view, no more than a version of a gesture of fellowship well known to social anthropologists – the exchange of gifts. It serves, that is, to express and strengthen the natural bond between Gawain and Bercilak, as well as fulfilling their artificial covenants. (Burrow, p. 95)

As Burrow's anthropological reference suggests, the basic concept of the Generous Host pre-dates the romance and, as one of its inheritances from folklore, carries with it narrative possibilities and thematic significances which are far from courtly. There is, most significantly, the usage of the shared or lent wife, a primitive 'act of fraternisation' of which Burrow sees hints in the seating arrangements at the Hautdesert feasts (1001–6, 1657–63), where Berilak sits with the elder lady and leaves Gawain to share the dishes set before his wife, and in the host's suggestion that, during his absence at the hunt, his guest shall remain '*wyth my wyf, þat wyth yow schal sitte / And comfort yow with compayny*' (1098–9) (Burrow, pp. 95–6). But if these references are felt to have that significance, they are scarcely reassuring since some husbands freely permit kisses but nothing more and others punish even the slightest familiarity with death. For the Generous Host may also be the Imperious Host who, though entertaining his guest hand- somely, demands absolute obedience while he remains under his roof to the social laws which govern their relationship and even to his own whims.[16] In folktale he appears as the humble peasant or charcoal-burner who entertains a king in disguise and, despite the differences in their rank, teaches him that 'charbonnier est maître chez soi'. In romance, as noble host, he punishes any breach of good manners, but treats courteous guests with generous hospitality. In both he demonstrates a fine point of medieval etiquette: it is ill-bred in a guest not to obey his host's every command or even to protest that he is too generous, since that would be to question the host's right to rule in his own house.[17]

This relationship between guest and host rests upon a social convention which, in *Sir Gawain*, is specifically established in almost legalistic terms and reinforced at various points during Gawain's stay at Hautdesert. As the Generous Host, Bertilak welcomes him with a formula which makes him master of the castle and all it contains:

> He sayde, 'ȝe ar welcum to welde as yow lykez
> Þat here is; al is yowre awen, to haue at yowre wylle
>   and welde.'   (835–7)

In return, Gawain fulfils his duty as a guest by concealing his private concerns and joining wholeheartedly in the Christmas festivities, for which his host thanks him on their conclusion

(1031–6). Gawain's reply acknowledges his duty to him in terms suggestive of the oath of a feudal dependent:

> 'And I am wyȝe at your wylle to worch youre hest,
> As I am halden þerto, in hyȝe and in loȝe,
>   bi riȝt.'   (1039–41)[18]

When, the holy-days being over, he wishes to renew his search for the Green Chapel and is persuaded to stay longer by being assured that it is near by, he again puts himself at his host's disposal:

> 'Now acheued is my chaunce, I schal at your wylle
> Dowelle, and ellez do quat ȝe demen.'   (1081–2)

This is in private but, immediately afterwards, Bertilak extracts a formal repetition of his service before witnesses:

> 'Ȝe han demed to do þe dede þat I bidde;
> Wyl ȝe halde þis hes here at þys onez?'
> 'Ȝe, sir, for soþe,' sayd þe segge trwe,
> 'Whyl I byde in yowre borȝe, be bayn to ȝowre hest.'
>   (1089–92)

It is in this context, socially relaxed yet with overtones of verbal formality, that Gawain agrees to lie late next day, assured of the Lady's company, and to the Exchange of Winnings compact (1105–12), quickly and casually introduced but couched in legal terminology and sealed with the binding ceremony of the shared drink. Introduced at the climax of a fitt in which his obligation to Bertilak as a dutiful guest has been so thoroughly established, refusal by Gawain of this innocent-seeming extension to the Christmas sports, with its echo of the game at Arthur's court in which kisses were exchanged for innocuous, anonymous *hondeselle*, seems unthinkable – even if he recalled that other compact for an equal exchange made during the festivities there, with which his hands are now *stafful*. His response is in keeping with the spirit of the season:

> 'Bi God,' quoþ Gawayn þe gode, 'I grant þertylle,
> And þat yow lyst for to layke, lef hit me þynkes.'
>   (1110–11)

Which, if either, *layk* at Arthur's court (*cf.* 283–4) is in his mind, the reader is left to judge. And the fitt ends on the ambiguity of the compact, with repeated restatement of the *forwardes* reminiscent of that earlier *gomen* (*cf.* 377–97):

> To bed ȝet er þay ȝede,
> Recorded couenauntez ofte;
> Þe olde lorde of þat leude
> Cowþe wel halde layk alofte.   (1122–5)

What this particular *layk* portends, the reader must decide for himself: a further instance of Bertilak's playful nature as the Generous Host? or a formal compact to be rigidly enforced by the Imperious Host?

These ambiguities as to the character of Bertilak, the role he is playing, and the compound of game and earnest in his compact with Gawain must colour our view of what happens in his absence and our expectation of his reaction to it on his return. When his hunting is interrupted by the Lady's pursuit of Gawain, we are likely to wonder whether he is complicit with her, either as the Generous Host putting his wife at a guest's disposal, or as the Imperious Host preparing to teach Gawain a lesson in the duty of guest to host. If a guest is duty-bound to defer to his host's will, does that obligation extend to the wishes of his host's wife? Gawain's response to the Lady's first assault might suggest that he recognises such an obligation to obey her: '*Me schal worþe at your wille, and þat me wel lykez*' (1214). It is a sound, all-purpose response for the dutiful guest as well as a non-commital acknowledgement of her use of the *prisonnier d'amour* conceit. But it proves something of an embarrassment when the Lady attempts to reverse the normal courtly love relationship by declaring herself his *seruaunt*, casting him in the active role of master rather than passively obedient 'man'. Her ambiguous formula:

> 'Ȝe ar welcum to my cors,
> Yowre awen won to wale,
> Me behouez of fyne force
> Your seruaunt be, and schale'   (1237–40)

seems to echo the words in which her husband made Gawain free of his castle and all it contains (*cf.* 835–7).[19] Throughout the rest of the interview, Gawain continues to acknowledge his submission to the Lady as the wife of his host:

> 'Bi God, I were glad, and yow god þoȝt,
> At saȝe oþer at seruyce þat I sette myȝt
> To þe plesaunce of your prys – hit were a pure ioye'
>
> (1245–7)

while striving to re-establish the proper male–female courtly love relationship – at a purely verbal level:

> 'And, soberly your seruaunt, my souerayn I holde yow,
> And yowre knyȝt I becom, and Kryst yow forȝelde.'
>
> (1278–9)

This double duty – to the Lady as woman and as his host's wife – and its dual interpretation – as deeds on her part and words on his – is the source both of the tension and of the humour which run through the scene.[20] Ironically, because of it, the absent husband is continuously present, both in Gawain's awareness of his duty to him and in his discreet reminder to the Lady that she is not a free agent (1276). Under the courtly surface of the scene lurks the common implication of bedroom scenes in fabliau: when will the husband return (Burrow, p. 75)?

And how will he interpret the kiss which represents Gawain's winnings after a day spent in the company of his wife? As a courtly man of the world recognising a social commonplace no more significant than the kiss exchanged in his presence at Gawain's first meeting with the Lady (970–4)? As the Generous Host content to share with his guest the favours of his wife? As the Imperious Host, happy that his guest has taken him at his word in making himself free of the castle and all it contains or – alternatively – furious that his hospitality has been abused beyond a predetermined limit known only to himself? If the rhetorical implications of the parallel hunt, the slaughter of the deer, the atmosphere of mingled pleasure and violence in the field, and the underlying tension in the bedroom lead us to expect an ominous outcome, what form might it take? From the Imperious Host all forms of violence are possible, but Bertilak is also *þe olde lorde of þat leude*, experienced in the social and – the Exchange of Winnings compact suggests – the legal forms of feudal society. By feudal usage, the proper recourse for him, should he interpret the kiss as evidence of sexual impropriety, is to arraign Gawain before his own seigniorial court, composed of his personal retinue, as one owing temporary allegiance to him while his guest.[21]

The possibility of a charge of felony, of breach of trust, must challenge the reader's judgement of Gawain's guilt or innocence, both in terms of the technicalities of feudal justice and of his own moral and chivalric code symbolised by the pentangle, that perfect figure devised *In bytoknyng of trawþe*. The meaning of *trawþe* for fourteenth-century audiences has been exhaustively analysed by John Burrow (pp. 42–5): rooted in 'the quality of being true' (*OED troth* n., I) and diversified in sense according to the principle, cause, person, quality adhered to; 'fidelity to others, to promises, to principles; faith in God; moral righteousness; personal integrity' (Barron, pp. 10–11). The balanced wholeness of the figure emphasises the inter-dependence of these qualities in the chivalric perfection to which the Pentangle Knight aspires: 'His virtues are so closely interlocked that a test of any one of them cannot help being a test of others as well. Conversely, a failure in one cannot help being also a failure in others' (Spearing, p. 209). Ever since he left Camelot bearing these arms, his *trawþe* has been at test: for fidelity to his compact to seek out the Green Knight; for chivalric integrity in facing the perils of the wilderness, natural and supernatural; for enduring faith in God through the godless solitude of the Wirral. And since the Lady's first entrance to his bedroom, it has become apparent that he is also under test in the apparent security of Hautdesert, most evidently for *trawþe* to the social virtues of the fifth of the pentangle's pentads: *clannes* (freedom from lust), by resisting the sexual implications of the Lady's advances; *cortaysye* (courtesy towards and consideration for others), in avoiding open offence to her by the form of his rejection; and *felaȝschyp* (loyalty to others), in observing a guest's duty not to abuse hospitality by infidelity with the wife of his host. The complexity of the social situation, involving Gawain in multiple, apparently conflicting obligations – to God, to the Round Table whose representative he is, to his personal honour, to his host and hostess – illustrates the moral complexity of the code by which he lives.

We might judge that, in everything he has done at Hautdesert, Gawain has perfectly fulfilled his obligations, moral, chivalric, and social, and maintained his *trawþe*. But what are we to make of the kiss? A trifling social concession? Yet for the Pentangle Knight any deviation from *felaʒschyp*, even for the sake of *cortaysye*, must distort his integrity and make *vntrawþe*. A technical breach only, devoid of moral significance, since Gawain's acceptance of the kiss seemed entirely passive? But have we the right to make moral judgements on the basis of social appearances alone? The thought of such judgements being made on such evidence by the returning hunters, without our knowledge of what passed in the bedroom, seems unjust, grotesque. Yet we have to admit that, within the conventions of romance, the kiss might furnish grounds for a charge of sexual treason.

When, therefore, instead of the return of the husband to court, we find him still in the field (1319–64), presiding amongst his followers at the *asay* of the quarry, we may see the metaphor of the hunt continued in the execution of the penalty for treason. If so, the term *asay* may be read as having a double sense: not only the highly technical meaning of 'examination of the venison for quality and condition', but also 'a testing of character or personal traits (such as faithfulness, friendship, faith, fortitude); trial, ordeal' (*MED assai* n., 2(*a*)).[22] The treatment of the bedroom scene has made clear that Gawain is aware of the dual obligation imposed on him by his reception at Hautdesert, of courtesy to the Lady and loyalty to her husband; that the sexual temptation is comparatively superficial and his chastity never seriously in danger; and that the issue between them on Bertilak's return will be Gawain's fidelity to the bond of friendship between host and guest, formalised by usage as a semi-feudal relationship.[23] Should *asay* suggest a formal trial, the technical charge might be sexual treason, but the moral basis of the crime, as indicated by the various attitudes to treason surveyed in the previous chapter, would be breach of trust, that *trawþe* between man and man which is fundamental to the many forms of feudal relationship. The brutality of the punishment would reflect the moral and social gravity of the felony, rather than the trifling nature of the evidence, the surrendered kiss.

The breaking of the deer bears only an outline resemblance

to the common form of execution for treason, in that the bodies of the animals are opened, their entrails removed, their heads cut off, the carcasses divided and distributed. But these are necessary and normal stages in the breaking process, the description is technically exact in conformity with the hunting manuals of the period (TGD, pp. 111–12), and there are details – such as the removal of the hide prior to dismemberment, the knotting of the gullet to prevent the contents of the stomach from spilling out, etc. – which can have no meaning in relation to the execution of traitors.[24] The animal butchery is merely suggestive of the legal ceremony in a general metaphorical way.[25] Certain details may be suggestive to some of parallels from which other minds will shrink away.[26] To contemporary imaginations, the atmosphere of ordered ceremonial calm might suggest the formal solemnity surrounding the public execution of some great nobleman found guilty of treason.[27] Atmosphere may, indeed, be as important in conveying the metaphorical import here as in the first half of the deer hunt. The congruity between the hunting there and the wooing which follows is no more detailed than that between the breaking of the deer and execution for treason, or, indeed, than is usually the case with the metaphorical hunt. What is, in any case, being implied is only a narrative possibility, sufficiently shocking to stimulate readers familiar with the metaphorical hunt and its often fatal outcome to consider the thematic implications, without, at this stage, committing the poet, whose use of tradition is so often superficially conventional and fundamentally ambiguous, to a particular interpretative line.

If the conformity of detail is sufficient to suggest that the wooing scene, like the chase in the forest, is to end in death, the death of a traitor, the poet's use of the metaphorical hunt will appear more meaningful and elaborately structured, much more ominous in its implications. Realisation of the extent to which Bertilak and his wife are one in their relationship to Gawain removes any difficulty as to how the Lady is to 'kill' her quarry as her husband kills his. As their guest he is bound to keep *trawþe* with both: with the Lady by observing the ambiguous concept *cortaysye*, though in words not deeds; with the lord in the fundamental matter of respecting his wife's honour and the comparatively trifling matter of observing the Exchange of Winnings compact. Should Bertilak interpret the kiss as a moral rather than a technical breach of the guest–host relationship and attaint Gawain of treason, the Lady, by prevailing upon Gawain to accept it, will have been the instrument of his death as surely as her lord. What at first sight appeared to be an instance of the amorous hunt will prove instead to be the mortal hunt.

In contemporary literature, fusion of one type of the metaphorical hunt with another is not uncommon, and most frequently the love chase supplies the basic pattern, as in the works of Chrétien, Chaucer, and Gottfried von Strassbourg.[28] In Chaucer's *Book of the Duchess*, as Professor Thiébaux interprets it, the hunt, though only briefly and sporadically mentioned, is both thematically and structurally important. By directing the dreaming poet to his meeting with the Man in Black it provides a frame to the latter's lament for the loss of his *faire White*. Thematically, by repeated word-play upon 'hart'/'heart', it associates the death of the stag with that of the beloved, the husband's *herte swete*, epitomising the twin theme of the elegy: 'love defined and perfected by death, death itself illuminated, made stately, its terror muted by the husband's love, and both love and death embraced within the Poet's vision'.[29] The hunting of the stag is literal, its contribution to the theme of the poem metaphorical; and its dual nature as the amorous and the mortal hunt is no more explicit than in *Sir Gawain*.

If the multiple tradition of the metaphorical hunt strengthened other indications that the Lady's amorous pursuit of Gawain might end in his death, what follows the ominous breaking of the deer is anticlimax and relaxation of tension in an atmosphere of warmth and goodwill:

> Wyth blys and bry3t fyr bette.
> Þe lorde is comen þertylle;
> When Gawayn wyth hym mette
> Þer watz bot wele at wylle.   (1368–71)

What passes between host and guest is not accusation and legal condemnation but fair exchange conducted in the language of commerce (1372–97). Bertilak's offering, impressive both in quantity and quality, is of substantial real value;

> ... al godly in gomen Gawayn he called,
> Techez hym to þe tayles of ful tayt bestes,
> Schewez hym þe schyree grece schorne vpon rybbes.
> 'How payez yow þis play? Haf I prys wonnen?
> Haue I þryaundely þonk þurʒ my craft serued?'
> 'ʒe iwysse,' quoþ þat oþer wyʒe, 'here is wayth fayrest
> Þat I seʒ þis seuen ʒere in sesoun of wynter.'   (1376–82)

The value of Gawain's return is more problematical:

> 'Tas yow þere my cheuicaunce, I cheued no more;
> I wowche hit saf fynly, þaʒ feler hit were.'
> 'Hit is god,' quoþ þe godmon, 'grant mercy þerfore.
> Hit may be such hit is þe better, and ʒe me breue wolde
> Where ʒe wan þis ilk wele bi wytte of yorseluen'
>
> (1390–4)

– the worth of a kiss depending on who gave it and in what spirit. The commercial terms in which the exchange is expressed (*tayles* ('tails'/'tallies' – Waldron, p. 89), *payez*, *prys*, *wonnen*, *craft*, *couenaunt* (1384), *worthyly* (1386), *cheuicaunce*, *wan*, *wele*) may seem improper between noblemen and foreign to the spirit of game in which it was originally undertaken – and which persists in the tone set and the vocabulary used by the lord (*in gomen*, *payez*, *play*, *prys*, *craft*). Knowing the circumstances in which the kiss was given – taken by the Lady rather than 'won' by Gawain, the reader will have formed his own opinion of its value and be disturbed by echoes from the verbal duel in which it was the ambiguous prize: *prys* ('personal worth'), to which the Lady gave amorous as well as financial overtones (*cf.* 1249–58; see above, p. 28), forcing Gawain to remind her that as a married woman she is not free to chaffer in the market for hearts (*cf.* 1276–9); *worthyly*, echoing Gawain's protestation that he was *wyʒe vnworþy* of the *reuerence*, the *worchyp* she sought to pay him (*cf.* 1241–4; 1263–7) (Burrow, p. 88).

In that contest Gawain had been faced with the alternatives of denying his identity ('*I be not now he þat ʒe of speken*' (1242)) to avoid conforming to a distorted interpretation of it, or of having the Lady challenge it ('*þat ʒe be Gawan, hit gotz in mynde*' (1293)) because of his refusal to conform to her misinterpretation. The kiss is a compromise on his part, a forfeit reminiscent of the festive kissing game at Camelot (see above, p. 32 n. 5), but in earnest of what? If in the Lady's eyes it is the first trophy in an amorous intrigue to be continued, then Gawain, in failing to respond to her husband's wish to know '*Where ʒe wan þis ilk wele*', is conforming to her distorted view by extending chivalric courtesy to include that secrecy which was enjoined in courtly love. By his discretion he has given a hostage to fortune. Should the Lady interpret the kiss as an earnest of future compliance with her view of his knighthood, Gawain, by interpreting *cortaysye* so generously, may have put other aspects of his chivalric integrity at risk, distorting his pentangle and calling his true identity in question. But as it is values that are at forfeit, the challenge is from within; there seems no risk from external forces, since Bertilak takes the kiss so calmly. True, there are uneasy undercurrents in his jocularity. His implication that the undisclosed source of the kiss might make it outweigh the rich trophy of game could suggest that, were the source publicly declared, he would not treat the kiss as a trifling matter; while his comment that Gawain won it '*bi wytte of yorseluen*' may be an ironic indication that he knows how passive he had been in the matter of kissing. These hints of hidden knowledge on Bertilak's part renew the puzzle of his relationship to the formulaic roles of Generous Host and Imperious Host, but his relaxed tone implies no immediate threat.

Despite an undercurrent of tension caused by uncertainty as to which of the various romance traditions evoked is really relevant here, earlier fears that the metaphorical hunt might end in a traitor's death must seem ludicrously exaggerated and unfounded. Of those readers who entertained them, some may now feel shamefaced that they misjudged the balance of game and earnest in the poem and be over-ready to accept the relaxed mood of the Exchange of Winngs scene at its face value; others, remembering the ambiguous atmosphere surrounding that other Christmas game which resulted in one beheading and the threat of another, may continue to be uneasy for Gawain's safety. The former will accept the renewal of the Exchange compact *in her bourdyng* (1398–1411) as part of the festive ritual; the latter may note its mixture of legal (*forwardez, couenauntez*) and commercial terminology (*cheuysaunce, beuerage*[30]), ominously formal for a mere wager between noblemen, wondering, perhaps, whether its renewal forbodes disaster like the restatement, by a severed head, of the terms of that earlier Exchange (*cf.* 444–53), and whether the dual pattern of the one will impinge in any way upon the expected triple pattern of the other.

Triple patterns of narrative repetition are familiar from folk-tale, in which the function of the second day is to confirm the events of the first in order and import. So it is in *Gawain*, but with some significant variations. The opening of the second hunt (1412–67) confirms Hautdesert as a place of courtly and Christian procedure, Bertilak as active leader (*Þe lorde watz lopen of his bedde*) of a vigorous company engaged in natural and healthy pursuits. As before, the excitement of the hunt is conveyed in terms of sound (1417, 1421–3, 1426–8, 1445–9, 1453, 1465–6), but always as raised by the hunters not as heard by the quarry (*cf.* 1148–53), and the only compassion excited on this occasion is for the savaged hounds who *Ful ʒomerly ʒaule and ʒelle*. This and the rugged, rocky landscape in which it takes place (1419, 1430–4, 1450–3) set the mood for the second hunt, in which the human pleasure and animal terror of the first is to be replaced by violence and danger on both sides.

The procedure of the boar-hunt is vividly detailed and technically exact, yet many of its features have such relevance to Gawain and his circumstances as to suggest an association with the quarry. The boar's lurking place is known to the hunters and he lies doggo there until they *bede hym vpryse* (1434–8); their quarry on this occasion is a single male beast, noble game, renowned as a fierce fighter, and long separated from the herd as Gawain from his Round Table companions (1439–44). The association is meaningful here, as it could not be in the opening phase of the first hunt, since we naturally expect a renewal of the Lady's pursuit of Gawain; but the ironic irrelevance of his military prowess in the face of such an attack can only seem mildly comic and emotionally confusing, like his initial deer-like timidity on that occasion. Yet the anticipated comedy is undercut by the implications which the pattern of the boar-hunt has for the coming encounter in the bedroom: the driven beast turning at bay, striking out fiercely

at those who bait him, their arrows rebounding ineffectually
from his tough hide but infuriating him to break through the
ring of his tormentors with disastrous consequences to them
(1445–63). The suggestion that Gawain at bay in his bed,
maddened by the Lady's barbed taunts, might use his
renowned strength to strike out blindly, has ominous implications for his reputation as the flower of courtesy. If this hunt,
like the first, is to be read metaphorically, it would seem that a
pattern of behaviour is being laid down for Gawain: resis-
tence and repulsion, as inconsistent with *trawþe* to the pentangle values as the panic and flight suggested by the deer-
hunt. As on that occasion, the emergence of Bertilak from the
throng of hunters signals the end of the first phase of the hunt
(1464–7; *cf.* 1174–7), but at a much earlier stage in the chase,
before the lord has come to grips with the quarry and the kill is
not yet in sight. Since at this stage his hunting suggests no
outcome for the Lady's wooing, our concern for Gawain may,
on this occasion, be less for his loss of life than loss of reputation. Yet our mood must surely be ambivalent: it was never
clear how the Lady could, in her own person, 'kill' Gawain,
but a method by which she might provoke him into dishonour
has just been suggested to us.

The transition to the bedroom takes place as before in
mid-sentence and there is the same rapid re-establishment of
the luxury of Hautdesert, the handsomeness of the knight at
ease in his bed, *grayþely at home*, and a hint of impending
attack by the Lady (1468–79):

> Ful erly ho watz hym ate,
> His mode for to remwe.   (1474–5)[31]

The furtiveness of her first entry cannot be repeated, since
Gawain is obviously alert and waiting for her; but there is a
certain coy intimacy in the way *Ho commes to þe cortyn, and
at þe knyȝt totes*, and the same disturbing laughter as she seats
herself on his bed. She immediately renews her wooing just
where it was broken off at her first visit by querying Gawain's
identity in the light of his failure to live up to his amorous
reputation, and extracts another kiss, as void of commitment
on his part as the first (1480–1507). The effect is to carry us
back to the moment of that first kiss and to the moral and

social issues raised by it, now, perhaps, with less anxiety for Gawain's safety, since Bertilak received it so calmly, but continuing concern for his reputation as the Lady returns to an attack whose ultimate motive is still unclear. The apparent motive is still seduction, ambiguously expressed as a lesson in knightly duty:

> '. . . I kende yow of kyssyng,' quoþ þe clere þenne,
> 'Quere-so countenaunce is couþe quikly to clayme;
> Þat bicumes vche a knyȝt þat cortaysy vses.'   (1489–91)

The role of teacher adopted by the Lady, implying greater experience on her part, puts Gawain at a psychological disadvantage, like her earlier pose as his courtly *seruaunt* (*cf.* 1239–40), with its element of role-reversal. Fully alert and in control of himself, Gawain avoids discourtesy by acknowledging the social and ignoring the sexual implications of her lesson:

> If I were werned, I were wrang, iwysse, ȝif I profered.'
> 'Ma fay,' quoþ þe meré wyf, 'ȝe may not be werned,
> ȝe ar stif innoghe to constrayne wyth strenkþe, ȝif yow lykez,
> ȝif any were so vilanous þat yow devaye wolde.'   (1494–7)

Socially their views are directly opposed: to Gawain an unwelcome advance would be unchivalrous (*wrang*); to the Lady it is the rebuff which would constitute uncourtly (*vilanous*) behaviour. As on the first day, she equates chivalry with love, and love with deeds rather than *luf-talkyng*; as before, he avoids discourtesy by not challenging her interpretation, implying instead that it does not apply to him by obliquely opposing the chivalry of Camelot to that of Hautdesert:

> '. . . þrete is vnþryuande in þede þer I lende,
> And vche gift þat is geuen not with goud wylle.'
> (1499–500)

His language acknowledges the Lady's invitation to rape, while the faintly sententious tone in which he declines it suggests his readiness to fall into the natural male role of teacher correcting an aberrant female. It is another triumph for his skill in *talkyng noble*, but there is something faintly ridiculous in his determined obliquity and the passivity with which he submits to the Lady's kiss, depriving it of all sexual significance:

'I am at your comaundement, to kysse quen yow lykez,
ȝe may lach quen yow lyst, and leue quen yow þynkkez,
    in space.'
    Þe lady loutez adoun,
    And comlyly kysses his face   (1501–5)

This decorous rape of the male is a far cry from the earlier
implications of the scene, and it is scarcely surprising that
recent critics have had difficulty in seeing Gawain in the role
of the boar apparently prescribed for him by the parallel hunt.
I would suggest that, like the deer, the boar typifies the role
which Gawain is *invited* to play (Gallant, p. 36; McClure,
p. 378), by the carefully contrived circumstances of his seclu-
sion with the Lady, by her direct invitation, and, we may
suspect, by the collusion of her husband. The dishonour
involved in playing such a part is sufficiently obvious to the
modern reader, but the medieval audience, familiar with
contemporary tradition on the boar in life and lore might see
deeper significance in the role and his refusal to play it. The
hunting manuals of the period stress the ferocity of the boar, a
'proud' beast, and describe the honourable method of killing
him on foot, with the sword, in terms which echo the encoun-
ters of epic heroes. The danger lay in his razor-sharp tusks,
and Marcelle Thiébaux, in her study of the traditions, shows
how they centred about the cruel mouth.[32] In the allegorised
manual *Les Livres du roy Modus*, the boar is treated as a
'*beste noire*', a sinner glorifying Anti-christ and, with specific
reference to the dangerous mouth, as a giver of evil counsels.
Professor Thiébaux traces this moralised conception of the
beast partly to his original role as a Germanic cult animal
associated with the forces of fertility and later, in the *chansons
de geste*, with heathen powers opposed to Christianity, and
partly to exegetical commentaries, derived from glosses on
Psalm LXXIX, 13f, which treated him as a ravager associated
with the devil.

In secular literature, his power as a symbol of evil, concen-
trated in the mouth, expresses itself sexually and verbally:
'Troilo, the hero of the *Filostrato*, dreams that a boar is goring
Criseida with his snout, while she not only appears unper-
turbed but manifests pleasure. Before long Troilo realizes
that the boar is his rival, Diomedo . . .' (p. 296). In the *Ovide*

Moralisé, Adonis, warned by Venus not to hunt the cruel, proud beasts such as boar and lion lest these sports lead him into idleness and voluptuous ways, disobeys and is killed by the swine which represents the luxury and lechery in which he has lived; 'The boar has become the killing sin, a projection of the lustful inclination within Adonis' breast' (p. 296). The same concept of the boar as an embodiment of sin and the enemy of love occurs in Remon Vidal's *La chace au mesdisans* (1338), where its destructive mouth is made to function as the instrument of slander against lovers. In it a vicious beast, once a rich and powerful man whose malicious gossip against a pair of noble lovers so injured them that the god of love transmuted him into a boar, is hunted by a rout of courtly men and women with a pack of hounds, allegorical abstractions representing virtuous qualities effective against the offence of which the boar is guilty, *Belacueil*, *Bonté*, *Honneur*, *Largesce*, *Courtoisie*, *Biauté* and *Pitié* amongst others. Exhausted and brought to bay, the boar makes his confession before he dies: ' "I am wounded and beaten. It would be useless for me to cry for Mercy or Courtesy, Candor or Good Faith. They are all against me, as are all the good things of love. Because of this and for my calumnies I must go down to deepest hell. From my youth, I have been perfidious" ' (p. 294). The amorous chase is most frequently concerned with the relationship of lover and mistress; here it is turned into the mortal chase for the punishment of the third character in the conventional love-poetry triangle, the *lauzengier* or mendacious gossip who betrays their secret out of envy:

For the backbiter, while still a man, was termed *lechierres*. It was concupiscence that aroused his envy and caused him to malign the lovers' good names, *leur bele et bonne renommé*, which meant their reputation for chastity. Once their sexual faultlessness is assailed by the shameless slanderer, they separate and it becomes impossible for them to live.

(p. 296)

This concept of the lustful boar as the enemy of courtly love through his violent and malicious mouth was apparently central to the tradition of the beast in medieval secular literature. Readers familiar with it might, I suggest, interpret the parallel hunt, which casts Gawain in the role of the boar, as implying two possible courses of conduct for him: to take the Lady's hint and play the ravisher, or, alternatively, to act the *lauzengier*, reject her courtly formulae with brutal words, betray her secret advances to others and eventually to her husband. Any danger of the first is already ended one-third of the way through their interview, when the Lady's gently-taken kiss seems to admit her failure to rouse him to rape and they turn to talk *Of druryes greme and grace* (1508–57). The tone, set by the Lady, is literary and its vocabulary technical: *lettrure*, *tytelet token*, *text*, *werkkez* ('deeds'/'literary works' – Waldron, p. 95). Her theme is love as the inspiration of knightly deeds and her authority the romances of chivalry. Or rather that form of the courtly romance, typified by Chrétien's *Lancelot*, in which the search for an absolute idealism exalted love above all other sources of chivalric inspiration. It is evoked by the Lady with an uncritical admiration which begs the reader's judgement of the doctrine itself, and in terms of its specialised literary vocabulary (*drury*, *blysse*, *boure*, *bountees*, *dalyaunce*), raising the issue of its relevance to life and to Gawain's situation in a romance where he has been called on to display the sterner virtues and has, so far, denied the amorous reputation acquired in the kind of text to which the Lady refers. There are suspicious elements in her appeal to literary authority: the ambiguous terms in which she refers to love (*þe lel layk of luf*; *trweluf craftes*) as though it were part of the Christmas sports; the naivety – real or feigned? – of her role as a *ʒonke þynk* eager for instruction by Gawain; the incoherence of her application of literature to life, reflected in her syntax, suggesting either genuine inexperience or consciousness of shaky logic. And, as before, the implication is that her interest is in action rather than mere *luf-talkyng*:

> 'I com hider sengel, and sitte
> To lerne at yow sum game;
> Dos, techez me of your wytte,
> Whil my lorde is fro hame.' (1531–4)

Gawain adheres resolutely to the verbal level of their interview, accepting it as a game (*gle*, *gomen*, *play*, *ese*) of literary rather than practical reference (*expoun*, *temez of tyxt*, *talez*). Sincerely or diplomatically, he flatters her superior knowledge in matters of love, refusing the role of tutor:

'To yow þat, I wot wel, weldez more sly3t
Of þat art, bi þe half, or a hundreth of seche
As I am, oþer euer schal, in erde þer I leue,
Hit were a folé felefolde, my fre, by my trawþe.'
(1542–5)

The oath, however casual, may suggest that Gawain's mind is on his pentangle, conscious that the *lele luf* (1516) which the Lady seems to expect of him would be disloyal to her husband (Burrow, p. 92). His use of *sly3t* in reference to *þat art* (echoing the Lady's *trwelufcraftes* – itself ambiguous) may be an implied rebuke, suggesting the deceitful nature of such love (Mills, p. 626). His determined politeness and renewed assertion of the formulaic role of *seruaunt*, rather than instructor in the *layk ofluf*, show him in control of himself and the situation (Burnley, p. 6). Exceptionally, the poet openly confirms the impression of a drawn match – but also that a deliberate testing of Gawain has underlain the laughter and verbal sparring:

Þus hym frayned þat fre, and fondet hym ofte,
For to haf wonnen hym to wo3e, what-so scho þo3t ellez;
Bot he defended hym so fayr þat no faut semed,
Ne non euel on nawþer halue, nawþer þay wysten
        bot blysse.   (1549–53)

The consciousness that in human affairs *blysse* often leads to *blunder*, as the poet initially reminded us (16–19), may heighten the sense of moral danger implicit in *wo3e* (a pun on 'woo' – TGD, p. 116/'woe' – Waldron, p. 96?), *faut*, and *euel* (Mills, p. 626). As so often at Hautdesert, judgement is inhibited by emotional ambiguity in an atmosphere of social relaxation and underlying concern; so here, *Þay la3ed and layked longe*, and the second kiss of the day is given with casual disregard.

The almost immediate return to the hunting field, the realisation that on this occasion the kill is still to come, the discovery that it results from a fierce, single-handed encounter between man and beast (1561–600) effectively shifts concern for Gawain from the passive wooing to the violent hunting, from the unsuccessful Lady to the victorious Bertilak, reviving our suspicion that he is the key to both hunts, the literal and the metaphorical. Having re-introduced him as leader of the chase (1561–2), the poet continues the characteristic pattern of the boar-hunt interrupted by the bedroom scene: the boar stands at bay until, infuriated by showers of arrows, he breaks out and is pursued until he turns again. When finally cornered beside a stream, he is so maddened that only the lord dares approach him, sword in hand, for the most courageous and approved form of the kill:

> Þe swyn settez hym out on þe segge euen,
> Þat þe burne and þe bor were boþe vpon hepez
> In þe wyȝtest of þe water; þe worre hade þat oþer,
> For þe mon merkkez hym wel, as þay mette fyrst,
> Set sadly þe scharp in þe slot euen,
> Hit hym vp to þe hult, þat þe hert schyndered,
> And he ȝarrande hym ȝelde, and ȝedoun þe water
>   ful tyt.   (1589–96)

The assault by the cornered foe, the *mêlée* in which they roll together, the sense of equally matched opponents, *Þat fele ferde for þe freke, lest felle hym þe worre*, the final surrender of the defeated, all suggest one of those epic duels between heroes, for whose valour the boar often serves as an emblem in medieval literature.[33] I would suggest that, in this particular context, the battle of man and beast was intended as a metaphor of the judicial process known as Trial by Combat.

Trial by Combat became part of English legal procedure after the Norman Conquest, but was gradually restricted and replaced by other forms of trial until, by the thirteenth century, it applied only in appeals of treason and felony.[34] Under it the accuser appealed the accused, stating the facts of the crime with which he charged him and offered to prove it by his body. The principals were gradually replaced as combatants, first by accepted witnesses on their respective sides, later by professional champions.[35] Under Edward III, however, the treason duel was revived within the Court of Chivalry, which initially had jurisdiction only over cases of treason originating outside the realm but gradually extended its jurisdiction until, under Henry IV, it became an acknowledged alternative to Parliament for treason appeals.[36] Under Richard II, Parliament had made several attempts to define its jurisdiction and prevent it encroaching on the common law, but there were several notorious cases under its procedures.[37] They distinguish the treason-duel from the original duel at law in several respects: appellant and defendant fought in their own persons; they fought in armour and, initially at least, on horseback, using spear and sword, not the spiked baton of the primitive trial by battle.[38] In this chivalric form, Trial by Combat must have been familiar to aristocratic audiences in the age of Richard II.

If, in such a combat, the accused was defeated, his felony had been proved upon him by the judgement of God and, if he had not died in the process, formal execution would follow.[39] The boar dies at Bertilak's hand, but the unlacing which follows (1601–18), while technically exact (TGD, p. 117), is even more suggestive than the deer-breaking of a traitor's death: a single, noble, male victim and a single, expert butcher; beheading followed by disembowelling and dismemberment of the body; the newly severed head set *on hiȝe*, then carried before the returning hunters, as the heads of traitors were displayed to the crowd and then exposed in some public place; the entrails flamed on the embers, as the traitor's bowels were traditionally 'burnt before his face' – in the former case for a practical purpose, the feeding of the hounds; in the latter as a symbolic degredation. The emblematic association cannot accommodate all details, but for audiences familiar with the metaphorical hunt and with the boar as the type of the traitor their dual significance might well be more apparent than to us.[40] If so, they must have appreciated the irony that the Pentangle Knight was seemingly threatened with a traitor's death at the hands of Bertilak, associated with the ominous Green Knight and, like the Devil himself, a hunter (Randall, p. 481; Thiébaux, p. 80), acting as the agent of divine judgement. The anxiety with which they anticipated the meeting of the two men would function not merely as a source of narrative tension, but as a stimulus to consider the justice of such a fate. They could scarcely find Gawain guilty of following the course of conduct suggested for him, of imitating the boar either in lust or as *lauzengier*. Yet there remain the ambivalent tradition of the Imperious Host, and the two kisses to be surrendered to Gawain's host on his return.

There are elements of tension in the Exchange of Winnings

scene (1619–47); in the lord's eagerness to see Gawain, his
calling him to receive his *feez* (with ironic suggestion of the
reward due to a vassal),[41] and their handling of the boar's
head, which, before the surrender of the kisses, must still
seem ominous for Gawain. Yet Bertilak speaks to him with
solace, the *goude ladyez* are summoned and the exchange
made with *laȝter myry*. As before, there is play upon the
worth of the goods exchanged: the boar is valued by Gawain,
not merely materially, but in terms of the prowess displayed
by Bertilak in killing such a beast: *And praysed hit as gret prys
þat he proued hade*. After such open generosity, Bertilak's
comment on the kisses seems equivocal:

> 'Ȝe ar þe best þat I knowe!
> Ȝe ben ryche in a whyle,
> Such chaffer and Ȝe drowe.'   (1645–7)

Praise, presumably, because Gawain has doubled his takings
in one day; but what is the value of such winnings in Bertilak's
eyes, and to what qualities does his *best* apply? By comparison
with his host and – in terms of the hunting metaphor – his
opponent, Gawain would seem to have diminished in *prys*
('personal worth'); yet the kisses have brought no charge of
breach of *trawþe*, merely an ironic quip.

The exchange is briefer than on the first day; the supper
which follows (1648–63) has been expanded (*cf.* 1400–1) to
re-establish the civilised good-order of Hautdesert, which the
Lady threatens to disrupt by renewing her bedroom seduction
in public:

> Such semblaunt to þat segge semly ho made
> Wyth stille stollen countenaunce, þat stalworth to plese,
> Þat al forwondered watz þe wyȝe, and wroth with hymseluen,
> Bot he nolde not for his nurture nurne hir aȝaynez,
> Bot dalt with hir al in daynté, how-se-euer þe dede turned
>   towrast.   (1658–63)

The contrast with their previous social converse *closed fro
fylþe* (1013), Gawain's concern at the open display of
behaviour with which he had dealt so cooly and competently
in private, and his persistence in that politeness toward the
Lady which his *cortaysye* dictates – even though, under the
husband's eyes, it might be misconstrued – externalise the

bedroom situation, his awareness of the risks inherent in his social compliance, and refusal to compromise his code in public any more than in private. Though the poet challenges our judgement of it by referring to the scene as 'play' (1664), the Lady's boldness and her husband's blindness or complicity bode ill for the morrow.

All the more reason for Gawain to decline the renewal of the Exchange of Winnings compact (1664–85), and when it is proposed, he seeks leave to depart for the Green Chapel, despite his earlier agreement with Bertilak to remain until New Year's morning (1068–82). His eagerness to be gone may arise from consciousness of his obligation under the Exchange of Blows contract; equally, it may suggest his uneasiness in the social situation at Hautdesert under the terms of the other exchange compact. Yet, assured again of the nearness of his goal, he agrees to stay without question. *Fela3schyp* and social tact explain his silence superficially, but the reader may be stimulated by foreboding to wonder why he asks no questions of his host about the Green Chapel. Does he see nothing significant in Bertilak's knowledge of a place which others had denied knowing (703–8)? Does he not connect his passion for games with the grim *gomen* proposed by the Green Knight? Does he detect no resemblance between the two festive compacts? These were questions raised by the relationship between guest and host as the triple pattern of hunting and wooing was about to start (1046–125; see above, pp. 46–7). They are sharpened now, as the third repetition is about to begin, by ominous words from Bertilak, who, swearing *'As I am trwe segge, I siker my trawþe'*, adds:

> '. . . I haf fraysted þe twys, and faythful I fynde þe.
> Now "þrid tyme þrowe best" þenk on þe morne,
> Make we mery quyl we may and mynne vpon joye,
> For þe lur may mon lach when-so mon lykez.'   (1679–82)

So Gawain has been tested by his host as well as by the temptation sensed behind the Lady's wiles; but is this one test or two? Has he been found *faythful* merely to his troth in the exchange compact or to a wider *trawþe*? Can Bertilak's *trawþe* be equated with Gawain's; is he being tested by his chivalric peer or by a representative of some more malign romance tradition? For whom does the ambiguous '"Third time lucky"' augur well: the tester or the tested? The fateful nature of this third day is underscored by echoes, in the last two lines of Bertilak's speech, of the *glad–heuy*, *begynne–ende* parallelism in the poet's warning to us, as the year began to run between the beheading at Camelot and the tryst at the Green Chapel (491–9), of man's vulnerability to time and fortune:

> A ȝere ȝernes ful ȝerne, and ȝeldez neuer lyke,
> Þe forme to þe fynisment foldez ful selden.   (498–9)

The last day of the dying year dawns fair and foul, the raddled clouds clearing as the sun rises. This natural – and ambiguous – omen, as the lord, *þat his craftez kepes*, goes through the familiar ritual of mass, a hasty meal, and mounting for the field, is the first of many significant variations on this third day, so often critical in the triple pattern of folk-tale (Davenport, p. 162). Much in the treatment of the hunt (1690–730) reproduces the effects achieved on the previous days: due order and technical exactness in following the hunting procedure appropriate to the particular game (TGD, pp. 118–20), the huntsmen and hounds dominating the opening movement in which Bertilak plays no individual role, and the atmosphere of the hunt being conveyed in terms of noise (1698, 1701, 1706, 1721–5) mounting to a crescendo like a natural disaster, *As alle þe clamberande clyffes hade clatered on hepes*. But on this occasion the sounds are all raised by the sight or scent of the quarry and serve to track him through the forest like an emanation of his pursuers' contempt, devoid of fear on their part (*cf.* 1441–2, 1452–3), and raising no compassion for him (*cf.* 1150–66).

For the quarry is the fox, ignoble game, vermin, unfit to eat, infamous in popular tradition as shrewd, malicious, greedy, destructive of other game, and, above all, a thief. Though the hunting manuals give instructions for catching him, the courtly romances show little interest in such mean sport. But his notorious habits, traditionally interpreted in terms of human behaviour in the *Roman de Renard*, gave the allegorists ample grounds to use him as a symbol of craftiness, pride and treachery, the type of Satan himself (Schnyder, pp.

66–7). Marcelle Thiébaux finds particularly significant for *Sir Gawain* his treatment in Henry of Lancaster's penitential *Livre des Seyntz Medicines* (1354), where his den is the human heart:

> Henry reminds the reader of the stench of the fox, comparing the fox's den, with its entrances, to the body and its orifices. Within is a corner, a man's heart, where the vixen [*Peresce*, Sloth] cohabits with the male, *Orgoil*, to bring forth their whelps, the five other mortal sins. Foxes hide in their dens during the day but range abroad by night, seeking their prey. Henry gives the meaning: the evil of the human heart is generally kept concealed from the world's recognition, but at night the vices issue forth privily to do harm.[42]

The allegorical tradition seems, however, to have no immediate bearing on the opening of the fox-hunt in *Gawain*, which is concerned with the characteristic behaviour of the animal as he twists and turns, doubling back on his tracks to confuse the hounds. There is no condemnation of his wiles, which are matched by those of the dogs (1700), each behaving in accordance with his nature. From the moment he is first viewed, the hunt is conveyed as experienced by him (Benson, pp. 194–5); his delight in his own skill as he *fyskez* before the hunters, his shock on coming upon the waiting hounds who cut off his retreat – *With alle þe wo on lyue / To þe wod he went away*. If, in the anticipated parallelism of hunting and wooing, this is the model for Gawain's behaviour, it is surely even more unthinkable for the Knight of the Pentangle than the rejected prototypes of deer and boar.

Unless, that is, this third day is to see unexpected variations in the bedroom scene (1731–871). It opens with the usual time connection, indicating simultaneity of action, and the familiar contrast of cold without, warmth within. Neither continuity nor contrast promises immunity indoors, and there is significant variation in the long description of the Lady's dress, which, with its jewelled hair-net and naked back and breast, emphasises her youth and beauty, threatening a renewal of her sexual attack:

> . . . þe lady for luf let not to slepe,
> Ne þe purpose to payre þat py3t in hir hert
>
> (1733–4)

Confident of Gawain's continued success in resistance, we may not reflect that we still do not know the nature of the Lady's love or the real *purpose* of her visits to Gawain. To what purpose does she now vary her usual stealthy approach by throwing open the window, dispelling the unhealthily cloistered atmosphere of the bedroom by letting in the outer world of vigorous activity.[43]

She accuses Gawain of sloth, but already the threat of the outer world has invaded the apparent security in which he has slept *holsumly* ('for the good of his health', ironically ambivalent – Waldron, p. 104), bringing troubled dreams:

> How þat destiné schulde þat day dele hym his wyrde
> At þe grene chapel, when he þe gome metes,
> And bihoues his buffet abide withoute debate more;
>
> (1752–4)

He throws them off at her entrance, only to be assailed by the danger within, for at the sight of her beauty *Wiȝt wallande joye warmed his hert*. Clearly he has never been impervious to her sexual assault, however well he may have concealed his feelings, as now, with *smoþe smylyng*. As it is renewed for the third time, the poet openly admits the danger of the bedroom situation – *Gret perile bitwene hem stod, / Nif Maré of hir knyȝt mynne* – and Gawain shows that he clearly recognised the multiple threat to his *trawþe* should he:

> Oþer lach þer hir luf, oþer lodly refuse.
> He cared for his cortaysye, lest craþayn he were,
> And more for his meschef ȝif he schulde make synne,
> And be traytor to þat tolke þat þat telde aȝt.   (1772–5)

In the context of the formally established relationship between Gawain and Bertilak as guest and host (see above, pp. 44–5), the use here of *traytor* seems to me exact, a technical term for one who breaks his feudal troth, and, if by adultery with his lord's wife, doubly a sinner, both against *clannes* and against the Christian basis of the feudal oath. Faced with the possibility of acting towards the Lady as a *vilain* (*MED crachoun* n., 'a worthless person, a slob'), or towards her husband as a *felon*, it is the latter which Gawain emphatically rejects in his mind ('*God schylde,' quoþ þe schalk, 'þat schal not befalle!*'), even as *With luf-laȝyng a lyt*, he courteously parries the advances which invite him to sin. Being privy to his inner thoughts draws us closer to him, as during his winter journey (see above, pp. 19–20), while his *luf-la3yng*, echoing the ambiguous laughter of the wooing scenes, underlines the disparity between the inner and outer man through three days of maintaining *cortaysye* towards the Lady and *fela3schyp* towards her lord. The *luf-talkyng* on this third day is almost perfunctory: an allusion, in terms which echo the Lady's reading of courtly literature, to the obligation to love where one is loved unless one has previously plighted one's troth (*folden fayth*) to another, and a denial on Gawain's part that he has any *lemman*:

> Þe kny3t sayde, 'Be sayn Jon,'
> And smeþely con he smyle,
> 'In fayth I welde ri3t non,
> Ne non wil welde þe quile.'   (1788–91)

There is a certain self-conscious smugness in his smiling and his swearing by the celibate St John (Tamplin, pp. 411–14) which suggests his confident mastery of the situation; undercut, however, by his consciousness of that prior commitment which has inhibited any amorous response from the beginning (*cf.* 1284–5). The reader is challenged to consider what that commitment, expressed in the Lady's terms as '*a leuer, þat yow lykez better, . . . þat yow lausen ne lyst*' may be: love of *trawþe*, of life, of self?

Faced with a refusal as absolute as *cortaysye* allows, the Lady admits defeat, strikes the appropriate literary posture ('*I may bot mourne vpon molde, as may þat much louys*'), and, with the second kiss of the day, rises to leave. With her must go any possibility of an amorous significance in the parallel hunt, leaving the reader to wonder to what tradition of the metaphorical hunt, the still indeterminate chase of the fox will prove to belong. But, as on the first day (*cf.* 1290–1), the Lady turns to deliver a Parthian shot, requesting a keepsake, if only a glove, '*þat I may mynne on þe, mon*'. The glove would probably suggest to readers of romance that the amorous attack was merely changing ground, from contention over deeds on one side and words on the other to a struggle over tokens, since a glove might readily be interpreted as a conventional love-gage and, if displayed, would identify the giver. That, no doubt, is why Gawain refuses it, but in terms which suggest a more courteous reason: he accepts the idea of a love-gage (*drurye*), as he had earlier adopted the language of the love-game, but pretends that its material value should match the worth (*honour*) of the recipient:

> 'Bot to dele yow for drurye þat dawed bot neked,
> Hit is not your honour to haf at þis tyme
> A gloue for a garysoun of Gawaynez giftez'   (1805–7)

And, he reminds the Lady, the nature of his mission deprives him of anything more fitting to offer her. Consciously or unconsciously, he has reverted to the image of barter used by her on the first day (1248–58; see above, pp. 28–9), equating his *honour* and *prys* with *garysoun oþer golde* (Mills, p. 628). She seizes the implication and, with her usual attempt at male–female role reversal, offers him, as *'hende of hyȝe honours'*, a jewelled ring *worth wele ful hoge*, and interprets his refusal as implying that its value would impose too great an obligation: *'ȝe wolde not so hyȝly halden be to me'*. She proffers instead the girdle she is wearing, of silk and gold, calling it *vnworþi* ('of little value' / 'not equal to the worth of the recipient'), and it too is emphatically rejected in a shower of negatives:

> And he nay þat he nolde neghe in no wyse
> Nauþer golde ne garysoun, er God hym grace sende
> To acheue to þe chaunce þat he hade chosen þere.
>
>   (1836–8)

The rejection, continued in direct speech, comes close to discourtesy (*'lettez be your bisinesse'*), before Gawain, reasserting the proper male–female relationship by declaring himself yet again the Lady's *seruaunt*, re-establishes the tone of formal *luf-talkyng*, the atmosphere of courtly game, which he has striven to maintain throughout their interviews.

Three tokens, three refusals; the pattern of this variation upon the daily pattern should be complete. But there is a variation within the variation, turning again upon worth: value of token and personal worth. As in the case of the ring, the Lady resolutely misinterprets Gawain's reason for refusing the girdle, implying that he thinks it unworthy of him and adding:

> 'Bot who-so knew þe costes þat knit ar þerinne,
> He wolde hit prayse at more prys, parauenture'
>
> (1849–50)

Once again, the choice of terms recalls the value she put upon Gawain on the first day when his *prys* (1249) was based upon his *costes* (1272), equated by her with *bewté and debonerté and blyþe semblaunt* (1273), comparatively superficial qualities in the Pentangle Knight and valued by her in purely material terms. The qualities inherent in her girdle are more precious than its gold, for whoever wears it:

> 'Þer is no haþel vnder heuen tohewe hym þat myȝt,
> For he myȝt not be slayn for slyȝt vpon erþe.'   (1853–4)

The terms used have a disturbing relevance to Gawain's present circumstances, a few hours away from being *Hadet wyth an aluisch mon* (683) and now, if not when it first appeared from beneath her mantle, the girdle's green and gold become significant, ominously recalling the Green Knight, his green and gold axe and the *chaunce* to which, in God's grace, Gawain is bound. Everything about it challenges the reader to consider the *costes* ('inherent qualities') and *prys* ('worth' – material and symbolic) of the girdle. To the Lady: a love-token which, if accepted by Gawain, would impose upon him the obligations of a courtly lover? – but, if so, how connected with the Green Knight? To Bertilak, if accepted by Gawain and surrendered to him: an indication of sexual misconduct, the first garment to be removed in a seduction, a trophy as essentially feminine – and ambiguous – as the Countess of Salisbury's garter? To the reader himself: a symbol of the Lady's repeated efforts to involve Gawain in a relationship, superficially courtly, covertly sexual, rendered ambiguous by the complexity of romance tradition, the possible complicity of the Lady's husband and the hints of his association with the Green Knight (see above, pp. 42–3); an ominous *lace* (MED *las* n., ld. (*c*) 'a cord used as a bond or fetter'; 4 'a net, noose or snare; *fig.* entrapment') in which the Lady may be seeking to ensnare Gawain (Hieatt, pp. 118–19), and which, his conduct throughout their interviews suggests, he will reject.

And to Gawain?

> Þen kest þe kny3t, and hit come to his hert
> Hit were a juel for þe jopardé þat hym iugged were:
> When he acheued to þe chapel his chek for to fech,
> My3t he haf slypped to be vnslayn, þe sle3t were noble.
>
> (1855–8)

As at an earlier moment of emotional crisis, the Lady's first entrance to his bedroom, we share Gawain's thoughts and, as on that occasion (see above, p. 12), they seem entirely human and natural, based on the instinct for self-preservation rather than on rational consideration of the situation and its moral implications, the thoughts of the man beneath the armour rather than the Pentangle Knight. As before, we are provoked to smile and then to identify the source of our amusement in the gap between reputation and behaviour, between code and practice (see above, pp. 21–2), in the disparity here between decisive rejection on theoretic grounds (the nature of his mission) and inarticulate acceptance on pragmatic grounds (the needs of his mission):

> Þenne he þulged with hir þrepe and þoled hir to speke,
> And ho bere on hym þe belt and bede hit hym swyþe –
> And he granted and hym gafe with a goud wylle –
> And biso3t hym, for hir sake, disceuer hit neuer,
> Bot to lelly layne fro hir lorde; þe leude hym acordez
> Þat neuer wy3e schulde hit wyt, iwysse, bot þay twayne
> for no3te;
>
> (1859–65)

The issues are stylistically underscored: the complacency of *þulged* and *þoled* after the brusqueness with which he had earlier silenced the Lady (*cf.* 1840–1); the formality of *granted*, echoing the pompous refusal of lines 1836–8 and undermined by the over-eager acceptance interjected into the Lady's offering speech before the governing condition of concealment is known; the over-ready agreement to that vital condition ironically echoing in its double negative the earlier emphatic refusal. And, as before, our amusement is undercut by concern for Gawain's well-being, physical and moral, by certain stylistic ambiguities: his sudden interest in the girdle as a *juel* ('godsend' – Barron, p. 127; *MED jeuel* n., 2(*a*)

'Something valued for religious, magical, or human reasons') may remind us that the magical powers attributed to jewels in the Middle Ages included harmful as well as helpful qualities – as the diamonds *þat boþe were bryȝt and broun* round his own helmet (615–18) might suggest (Blanch, p. 75); *þe sleȝt were noble*, echoing the dubious *slyȝt* ('stratagem') felt to underlie the Exchange of Blows compact, and referring ambiguously to the girdle ('device') and the trick by which it might operate, queries its fittingness for a nobleman; the rapidity with which Gawain *hym gafe* recalls his readiness to echo the Lady's *prisonnier d'amour* conceits (1214–21; *cf.* 1210–11, 1224–5) – used there as part of the social game of *luf-talkyng*, but here in deadly earnest?; and equally, what Gawain has promised to *lelly layne* from her husband seems inconsistent with his rejection of the Lady's *lel layk of luf* (1513) as an act of treason against Bertilak (1775), under-scoring the nature of his surrender and the apparent impossibility of continuing to be loyal to both husband and wife. More ominously still, once we are made privy to Gawain's consciousness we find there the language of the fox-hunt – *kest, chek, slypped* – and realise that the approved *sleȝt* by which death may be avoided echoes the *wylez* by which the fox tries to escape the hounds. It may dawn upon us that, from the Lady's first assault as he *lay lurked* in his bed, there has been much of the fox in Gawain's behaviour: deceptively pretending to sleep, feigning to waken, profaning the sign of the cross to support his pretense, skilfully dodging the Lady's verbal traps, continually doubling back to his stance as courtly *seruaunt*, indulging in *luf-talkyng* without love, playing the game but with fear of death at his heart. And as we watch him now, earnestly thanking the Lady, receiving the third kiss of the day as she leaves, then rise and:

> Lays vp þe luf-lace þe lady hym raȝt,
> Hid hit ful holdely, þer he hit eft fonde.   (1874–5)

we may remember that, by tradition and during the lord's hunting, the fox was *ofte þef called*.

Gawain passes the remainder of the day with even greater contentment than usual and we return to the still indeterminate fox-hunt (1894–923). The fox is still running well, but

Bertilak has outstripped him and is about to head him off:

> And braydez out þe bryȝt bronde, and at þe best castez.
> And he schunt for þe scharp, and schulde haf arered;
> A rach rapes hym to, ryȝt er he myȝt,
> And ryȝt bifore þe hors fete þay fel on hym alle,
> And woried me þis wyly wyth a wroth noyse.   (1901–5)

If the metaphorical hunt is still felt to be operative, the implications for Gawain are ominous: that starting back from fear of death under the Green Knight's axe he may fall into the hands of his pursuers. By what legal process? The presentation of the hunt in terms of the sounds of pursuit, the term *rabel* (*OED rabble* n. 1, A 1 'a pack, string, swarm (of animals)'; 2 'a mob') applied to hounds and huntsmen, their denunciation of the fox (1706) and the curses *þay sette on his hede* (1721), their threats and cries of 'thief' (1725), the long chase through the wood and the hunters in ambush round it, all suggest the hue and cry: 'When a felony is committed, the hue and cry (*hutesium et clamor*) should be raised. . . . The neighbours should turn out with the bows, arrows, knives, that they are bound to keep and, besides much shouting, there will be horn-blowing; the 'hue' will be 'horned' from vill to vill.'[44]

The characteristic crimes pursued by the hue and cry were murder and robbery; robbery was originally distinguished from theft, which, as a secret crime, was regarded as far more dishonourable.[45] By concealing the girdle, Gawain may have laid himself open to the graver charge. Medieval readers would recognise the implications, should the returning hunters find it in his possession:

Now if a man is overtaken by hue and cry while he has still about him the signs of his crime, he will have short shrift. Should he make any resistance, he will be cut down. But even if he submits to capture, his fate is already decided. He will be bound, and, if we suppose him a thief, the stolen goods will be bound on his back. He will be brought before some court (like enough it is a court hurriedly summoned for the purpose), and without being allowed to say one word in self-defence, he will be promptly hanged, beheaded or precipitated from a cliff, and the owner of the stolen goods will perhaps act as an amateur executioner.[46]

With each succeeding day and the mounting toll of kisses, the legal procedures suggested by the metaphorical hunt have regressed from the courtly to the primitive, from due process to rough justice, from ceremonious execution to a brief and brutal act of mob violence. Behind the seeming lynch law of the hue and cry lies the ancient conception that the criminal taken in the act was *ipso facto* an outlaw: 'He is not entitled to any "law", not even to that sort of "law" which we allow to noble beasts of the chase.'[47] The outlaw, like the wolf with a price on his head, may die at any man's hand. The fox, dead or dying, is snatched by Bertilak from the mouths of the hounds:

> And syþen þay tan Rèynarde,
> And tyruen of his cote.   (1920–1)

If the implication of the deer and boar hunts has been that Gawain stood in danger of the traitor's death of disembowelling, beheading and quartering, this must, I think, mean that he is now threatened with the rare but notorious penalty of flaying alive, which, the records suggest, was more likely to result from mob violence than formal legal process.[48] The thought of such a barbarous act at the civilised court of Hautdesert seems as untenable as the judicial pursuit of a nobleman by the hue and cry. But the fate of the de Launoy brothers (see below, p. 76, n. 7) shows how a sophisticated society could give way to barbarity in the face of breach of its sexual taboos and its feudal bonds, and the reign of Richard II provides many examples of the law of treason used irregularly in revenge against great nobles.[49] Medieval readers must have been uneasily conscious, ever since the beginning of the bedroom scenes, of the legal provision which made it not only a right but a duty for a husband to take summary vengeance, even on mere suspicion of adultery with his wife.[50] They may well have feared, remembering the ambiguous role of the wayside host in romance, that the whole business of hunting and wooing had been devised to entrap Gawain in *flagrante delicto* or circumstances justifying his execution.[51]

So far, however, the metaphorical hunt has been used, not to predict narrative developments, but to draw attention to inherent moral and thematic possibilities. The shocking implication of the flaying of the fox must prompt us to consider what crime on Gawain's part might expose him to such an extreme penalty. Sexual treason? – since, on this occasion, there will be three kisses to surrender to Bertilak, and, if Gawain honours the Exchange of Winnings compact above his promise of secrecy to the Lady, the *luf-lace* also. But, though the evidence of amorous intrigue is weightier and more concrete than on previous days, it is essentially of the same kind and no more genuinely proof of sexual impropriety than that which has been so jocularly received by the lord on those occasions. Theft? – since, should he retain the girdle, either for his own protection or that of the Lady's reputation, he will be withholding what properly belongs to Bertilak. But though theft is a felony, such a trifling theft scarcely warrants the extreme penalty for treason. Breach of *trawþe*? – towards his host, should he retain the girdle; towards his hostess, should he surrender it. But what treason does breach of the pentangle constitute? Treason to self, by falling short of self-imposed aspirations? To man, in neglecting those chivalric obligations which govern social relations in a feudal society? To God, in sinning against the fundamental Christian bond between man and his creator on which feudalism, chivalry, and Gawain's pentangle ultimately rest?

NOTES

1   R. H. Bloch, *Medieval French Literature and Law*, Berkeley, Cal., 1977, p. 4.

2   Having treated treason and its penalties at some length elsewhere ('A propos de quelques cas d'écorchement dans les romans anglais et français du Moyen Age', in *Mélanges Jeanne Lods*, Paris, 1978, pp. 49–68 and in 'The Penalties for Treason in Medieval Life and Literature', *The Journal of Medieval History*, 7 (1981)), I shall only outline here those aspects which are most relevant to *Sir Gawain*.

3   'Tresun est un chescun damage qe hom fet a escient ou procure de fere a cely a qi hom se fet ami' (*Britton*, ed. F. M. Nichols, Oxford, 1865, I, p. 40). 'Treason is a crime which has a vague circumference, and more than one centre. In the first place, there is the centre that is to this day primarily indicated by the word *betray*.' 'The bond of fealty is another centre. To betray one's lord was already in Alfred's day the worst of all crimes; it was the crime of Judas; he betrayed his lord' (Sir. F. Pollack and F. W. Maitland, *The History of English Law before the Time of Edward I*, 2nd. edn., Cambridge, 1968, II, p. 503).

4   Pollock and Maitland, II, p. 500. They add: 'This is the origin of that "drawing" which forms the first part of the penalty for high and petty

treason. The malefactor was laid on the ground and tied to a horse which dragged him along the rough road to the gibbet.' 'In course of time the law was not content with this in the graver cases of high treason. It demanded drawing, hanging, disembowelling, burning, beheading, quartering' (pp. 500–1).

5   Witness the fate of the Welsh and Scottish patriots who rebelled against Edward I: '. . . David of Wales was drawn for treason, hanged for homicide, disembowelled for sacrilege, beheaded and quartered for compassing the king's death. So Wallace was drawn for treason, hanged for robbery and homicide, disembowelled for sacrilege, beheaded as an outlaw and quartered for divers depredations' (Pollock and Maitland, II, p. 501, n. 1). The element of moral symbolism is still evident in the speech of Sir Edward Coke, as Attorney General, at the Gunpowder Plot trial in 1605: 'Then is he to be cut down alive, and to have his privy parts cut off and burnt before his face as being unworthily begotten, and unfit to leave any generation after him. His bowels and inlay'd parts taken out and burnt, who inwardly had conceived and harboured in his heart such horrible treason. After, to have his head cut off, which had imagined the mischief. And lastly his body to be quartered, and the quarters set up in some high and eminent place, to the view and detestation of men, and to become a prey for the fowls of the air' (*Cobbett's Complete Collection of State Trials*, II, London, 1809, p. 184).

6   '. . . sachés que non pas tant seulement doivent souffrir les faiseurs peine de traytre comme estre tonnelez et esquartelez ou escorchiez et tout le leur perdu et appliquié au seigneur, mais aussi leurs enfans, s'ilz les ont, doivent estre tournez en exil et a desert pour mort convenable. Et la rayson si est que tant horrible et detestable si est le crime de traytre, que de sa nature il infectue la semence du faiseur, et pour ce doit estre destruite la racine, estoc et semence. . .' (J. Boutillier, *La Somme rurale*, Paris, 1488, f. 91 v).

7   The case in which the brothers Philippe and Gauthier de Launoy, found guilty of adultery with two daughters-in-law of the king of France, Philippe-le-Bel, were publicly executed in 1314 by being flayed alive, emasculated, and hung on the common gibbet, made such an impression that it apparently inspired one of the warning tales in *Le Livre du Chevalier de la Tour-Landry*, written for the moral guidance of the *chevalier*'s daughters, of which Caxton made a popular English translation. Such sexual treason was felt to threaten the legitimacy of the royal succession.

8   For detailed references to these instances see Barron (1978), p. 51, notes 3–6 and p. 63, n. 44.

9   See *ibid*., pp. 63–7 and notes 45, 46, 49–51 and 53.

10   See *ibid*., pp. 52–3 and notes 8–10.

11   There is an obvious intention in lines 180–98 to associate the Green Knight with his horse through the hairiness of man and beast as well as their unnatural colouring. Whatever significance such an association had for contemporary readers might equally be evoked by Bertilak's beaver-hued beard.

12   The use of laughter throughout the poem is complex. The Green Knight's mocking laughter is ironic, since it expresses his awareness of the disparity between the Round Table's reputation for valour, which has provoked his appearance as Knight-challenger, and its stunned reaction to his challenge. Bertilak's laughter on learning who his guest is may be similarly intended, suggesting something in addition to the pleasure of entertaining a noble stranger – delight in the arrival of an expected victim? amused anticipation of his predicament? Any suspicions aroused as to the source of his private amusement may cast doubt on the sincerity of his boisterous mirth over the Christmas games, especially if we note how he laughs on hearing that Gawain is bound for the Green Chapel (1068), how his mood infects Gawain until *gomenly he la3ed* (1079) on hearing that his host knows its whereabouts (without wondering how or what he knows of it), and how they laugh together (1113) in concluding the Exchange compact which so closely resembles the grim bargain made with the Green Knight.

13   '. . . one must feel that Gawain's ignorance of his host's name involves ignorance of "the man", and further that this ignorance is a potential source of advantage to the host and danger to the hero' (Burrow, p. 60).

14   The balance of elements is no doubt dictated by the fact that, since so much in Bertilak's role as lord of a second Camelot suggests the parallel with Arthur, it is those aspects of his character reminiscent of the Green Knight which need to be stressed.

15   '. . . the Green Knight as well as Bertilak . . . are presented in a quite positive way when we first meet them, and it would be a simplification to explain this fact merely as the difference between appearance and reality, in fact the narrator intentionally refrains from any explicit comment or evaluation which would detract from the intriguing ambivalence and openness of the action' (Mehl, p. 198).

16   On the characteristics of the Imperious Host theme in romance, see A. Kurvinen, ed. *Sir Gawain and the Carl of Carlisle*, Helsinki, 1951, pp. 83–4.

17   The folk-tale versions are analysed by H. M. Smyser, '*The Taill of Rauf Coilyear* and its Sources', *Harvard Studies and Notes in Philology and Literature*, XIV (1932), pp. 135–50; Kittredge (pp. 76–106) considers the possible influence of romance versions on *Gawain*.

18   Some editors (Gollancz, Cawley, Waldron) put commas before and after *wy3e*, treating it as a term of address; the legal sense of the context seems to me (*cf.* TGD) best rendered by taking it as 'man, dependant'. Burrow (p. 67, n. 39) notes that *in hy3e and in lo3e* is a legalism corresponding to the Latin formula *in alto et basso*.

19   The echo is more apparent if, as suggested by Waldron (p. 169), we detect a pun on *won* meaning both 'take your own pleasure' (Waldron, p. 83) 'do as you like' (TGD, p. 109) and 'find your own dwelling' – with sexual implications?

20   For contemporary readers the implications may have been shar-

pened by a lingering awareness that the model for the courtly love relationship of male adoration of the sovereign lady was originally provided by the feudal relationship of lord and vassal, which also furnished some of its terminology, notably *midons* ('my lord') for the object of adoration.

21   Judgement by peers was introduced into England as part of Norman feudalism, in order to involve in thè judicial process those who would have to enforce the decisions of royal and seigniorial courts (see B. C. Keeney, *Judgment by Peers*, Cambridge, Mass., 1949, pp. 4–5). But under Henry II the powers of baronial courts were restricted by royal supervision: 'The control was so effective that Glanvill could wonder if a lord might distrain his own vassal to appear in his court for treason without a royal writ' (*ibid.*, p. 47). Maillart's *Roman du Comte d'Anjou* provides an example of such a treason trial under royal warrant in early fourteenth-century France (see above, p. 39). Such a trial, especially of one not formally a vassal of the seignior, seems improbable at the date of *Sir Gawain*: but what is the date of Arthur's empire, and in whose royal jurisdiction is Hautdesert? The English romances in general, though showing a keen interest in legal technicalities, often reflect somewhat antiquated usage, due partly to their use of outdated French sources, partly to the slowness with which new legal principles came into common practice (see O. Kratins, 'Treason in Middle English Metrical Romances', *Philological Quarterly*, XLV (1966), p. 681 and p. 687).

22   Readers might be reminded of the similar word-play on *tried* (4), implying both 'tried (for crime)' and the testing which determines 'of proven quality, distinguished, famous' (Barron, p. 167).

23   '. . . as Gawain knows, one owes a special loyalty to his host' – especially in regard to the women of his household. 'In the many medieval examples of the "Potiphar's Wife" tale, to which *Sir Gawain* is related, the tempted knights repulse the ladies not because of chastity but because of loyalty to the lady's husband' (Benson, p. 44). Not all romance heroes, however, are so loyal: 'Of all treasonable offences, unlawful carnal knowledge is charged most frequently in the romances' (Kratins, 'Treason in M.E. Romances', p. 671).

24   There is a basic dissimilarity in that the deer are dead before the ceremony begins, while the traitor who was to be disembowelled before beheading would first have been briefly suspended and, if fortunate, would still be insensible.

25   There does not seem to me to be any element of allegory in the parallel, any more than elsewhere in *Sir Gawain*. *Cf.* Burrow, p. 121; Mills, M., pp. 490–1.

26   The feeding of the hounds with the liver, lights and blood of the deer (1359–61) may raise memories of the fate of Jezebel (2 Kings IX, 35–7), the throwing of the *corbeles fee* into the bushes (1355) of the related prophecy that 'him that dieth in the field shall the fowls of the air eat' (1 Kings XXI, 24), both suggesting the element of divine retribution in judicial execution as well, perhaps, as gruesome, realistic details of what was a public spectacle in medieval life.

27   The modern imagination cannot associate ceremony with either form of butchery, but the Middle Ages appreciated its function in creating the awe appropriate to feudal justice and chivalric sport. A late but characteristic example of the ritualisation of punishment for offences against the royal security or dignity is provided by an act of Henry VIII prescribing loss of the right hand for murder or bloodshed within the king's court. Each stage of the ceremonial mutilation was under the supervision of some royal officer technically qualified by his domestic duty: the Serjeant of the Woodyard provided the chopping-block, the Master Cook the knife, the Serjeant of the Poultry a live cock in whose body the severed stump was to be wrapped until the Serjeant Farrier had sealed it with searing-irons; the Groom of the Salcery stood by with vinegar and cold water in case the victim should faint. (See. L. O. Pike, *A History of Crime in England*, London, 1873–6, II, p. 83.) Compare the following: '. . . venaison maie not be dismembred but of a gentilman; who bareheadded, and set on knees, with a knife prepared properly to that vse, . . . cuttes a sunder certaine partes of the wildbeast, in a certaine order verie circumstantly. Whiche duryng, the standers by, not speakyng a worde, behold it solemnly, as if it were some holy Misterie . . .' (Sir. T. Chaloner, *The Praise of Folie*, ed. C. H. Miller, EETS 257, London, 1965, p. 54).

28   See Thiébaux, *Stag of Love*, p. 12 and pp. 105–43.

29   *Ibid.*, p. 116.

30   Waldron (p. 78) notes that *beuerage*, from its use for the pledging drink in which bargains were sealed, itself acquired the technical sense 'bargain' in ME (*cf. MED*, 1(b)).

31   Concern as to her motive in these visits may be revived by the deliberate ambiguity of *mode* and *watz hym ate* ('she visited him'/'was pestering him' – Waldron, p. 93).

32   Marcelle Thiébaux, 'The Mouth of the Boar as a Symbol in Medieval Literature', *Romance Philology*, XXII (1968), pp. 281–99.

33   'The boar emblem, a sign of force, need not . . . be identified with the side of the battle that engages the audience's sympathies. And it is a question of which side bears the ensign or epithet, the hero or his adversary, that determines whether the boar is meant to indicate a mettlesome temper or a malignant one' (Thiébaux, 'The Mouth of the Boar', p. 286). For examples ranging from the *Nibelungenlied* to Chaucer's Knight's Tale, see pp. 285–7. *Cf.* Burnley, p. 7; McClure, p. 380.

34   See George Neilson, *Trial by Combat*, Glasgow, 1890, p. 36.

35   *Ibid.*, p. 47.

36   See G.D. Squibb, *The High Court of Chivalry*, Oxford, 1959, pp. 25–6.

37   In 1398, Henry, Duke of Hereford, appealed the Duke of Norfolk of high treason before Parliament; the lists prepared at Coventry were surrounded by a wet ditch or moat. When Henry, Earl of Essex, was appealed of treason in 1163, the combat took place on an island in the Thames at Reading (see Neilson, *Trial by Combat*, pp. 190–1 and p. 61). Is this isolation of the combatants, a distant echo of the Scandinavian *hólm-*

ganga, perhaps reflected in the struggle between the boar and Bertilak, who *Foundez fast þurȝ þe forth þer þe felle bydez* (1585) to join in single combat, *boþe vpon hepez / In þe wyȝtest of þe water* (1590–1)?

38 See Neilson, *Trial by Combat*, pp. 188–90.

39 'If the appeal was one of treason, the vanquished party, whether he was the appellant or the defendant, was disarmed in the lists and drawn behind a horse in the charge of the Marshal to the place of execution, where he was beheaded or hanged' (Squibb, *Court of Chivalry*, p. 23).

40 'The boar's defiance against the will of the god and goddess of love is put into terms that indicate treason; the most frequent epithet attached to the boar is *félon*, and he is *traître puans*, *vil cuivart*, *desloyaus*, *faus*, *honnis*, and *chétif* as well. His death, therefore, decreed by the God's authority, is consummated with religious fervour' (Thiébaux, 'The Mouth of the Boar', p. 297). In *La chace aus mesdisans* some details of the unlacing are given emblematic significance: 'The Count will have the head to display, but as for the sharp and hypocritical tongue, it must be pierced through with a sharp sword. The false, proud heart, along with the poisonous entrails, is to be burnt in a hot fire since they must not endure on earth' (*ibid.*, p. 294).

41 Though the sense thought appropriate here is 'Something given or due as a share of spoils or as a reward or prize' (*MED fe* n. 2, 6(*a*)), the word is a technical term in feudal law and many of its senses reflect feudal obligations. See K.-J. Hollyman, *Le Développement du vocabulaire féodal en France pendant le haut moyen âge*, Paris, 1957, pp. 41–55.

42 Thiébaux, *Stag of Love*, pp. 82–4. Elsewhere (Thiébaux (1970)), she suggests that the *Gawain*-poet may well have been influenced by the *Livre des Seyntz Medicines*.

43 The variation, reminding readers of the traditional contrast between the virtuous activity of hunting and the danger of lying long in bed, conducive to sloth and lust (Thiébaux, *Stag of Love*, pp. 75–80), may be intended as an ironic underscoring of the conventional perils of the bedchamber just when they are about to be supplemented by a greater temptation involving another form of sloth (see below, p. 97). Hughes (p. 230) sees this, Gawain's vivid awareness of impending death, and his strong physical attraction to the Lady as signs of reality breaking in upon the games of Hautdesert in preparation for his yielding to an instinctive impulse to save his life.

44 Pollock and Maitland, II, pp. 578–9.

45 *Ibid.*, pp. 493–4.

46 *Ibid.*, p. 579.

47 *Ibid.*, p. 580.

48 Witness, in English history, the fate of Hugh de Cressingham (see Barron (1978), p. 58). It is significant that Chaucer should liken the hue and cry after the thievish fox in the Nun's Priest's Tale to Jack Straw and his *meynee* slaughtering the Flemings during the Peasants' Revolt (see *Canterbury Tales*, VII, 3394–7).

49 See A. Steel, *Richard II*, Cambridge, 1941, pp. 132–4; pp. 154–7; pp. 226–7; pp. 234–9.

50 'According to medieval customary law, if a man captured his wife in a compromising situation with another man, he had the right to slay both wife and lover without risk to himself.' 'He need only raise the public cry – *le clameur de haro* – in order that the deed be known. The slaying must take place immediately, however, for the man who did not kill his adversary on the spot could later be prosecuted for murder' (Bloch, *Medieval Law,* pp. 55–6).

51 Amongst other instances in romance, they might recall the notorious entrapment of Lancelot in Guinevere's bedroom in *La Mort Artu* (see Bloch, *Medieval Law*, pp. 58–62).

III TREASON TO WHOM?

If, within the context of the metaphorical hunt, the flaying of the fox has ominous implications, they mark the climax of a dual development throughout the last three days of Gawain's stay at Hautdesert. The lord's hunting is characterised by the increasing effort involved on each occasion (Hunt (1976), p. 12) coupled with a progressive decline in the scale of the sport, the nobility and material value of the prey taken, and the ceremonial of its dismemberment (Henry, pp. 188–93). The Lady's wooing results in a corresponding narrowing of focus and reduction in dignity, increasingly concerned with Gawain's reputation, his initial return of compliment diminishing as his passivity and introversion grow, until there is something very like vanity in his *smoþe smylyng* and his suggestion (1806–7) that the glove she has begged as a keepsake would hardly be an adquate gift from such as himself (Henry, pp. 190–3; Spearing, p. 204). This process of growing social confidence and declining self-awareness is paralleled, if I am right in my interpretation of the metaphorical hunt, by more and more summary forms of the judicial process, ending in increasingly shameful forms of the traitor's death. Critics have sensed the threat behind both the Lady's blandishments and the ritual slaughter of the hunt: 'Death and moral danger go hand in hand in this section of the poem' (Hunt (1976), p. 12; *cf.* Spearing, p. 218). On the third day, the brief and brutal killing of a fox evokes a similar sense of betrayal of the expectations raised by the ceremonial of previous days, as does Gawain's apparent yielding to temptation after such a prolonged and courteous resistance (Burnley, p. 3). There now seems general agreement that the poet intended an analogy between the hero's behaviour on that occasion and the devious tactics of the fox as he tries to escape from his

pursuers with the fear of death in his heart (McClure, p. 375).
But there remains a wide disparity of opinion on the significance of Gawain's association with the fox, the implications of
its fate for his own at the Green Chapel, and the nature of the
fault which might merit such an end.

I am not alone in feeling that the variations in this third
repetition of the daily pattern indicate a change in the operation of the analogy (Barron (1973), pp. 15–16), from the
disparity between Gawain's behaviour and the roles suggested for him by deer and boar to the surprising congruity of
the fox's wiles with his devious behaviour in the bedroom
(McClure, p. 375).[1] But how far was the positive analogy
intended to go, and which aspects of the fox's reputation were
to be exemplified in Gawain? The Exchange of Winnings
game has been seen as essentially a test of his truth to his
pledged word, and the fox as a symbol of his ultimate
trecherye (McClure, p. 376); the flaying of the fox as the
stripping away of chivalric externals baring the hero's inner
nature (Hughes, p. 231); and the beast's *cote* as the counterpart of Gawain's *cote-armure* bearing the pentangle, which he
has now lost the right to wear 'precisely because he has feared
for his skin and betrayed himself by over-attention to the
identity signified by his *conysaunce*' (Henry, pp. 193–4). Such
interpretations, however, pre-judge Gawain's intentions with
regard to the girdle which, at the moment of the flaying, we
can interpret only by our reading of the third wooing scene
from the moment when the *luf-lace* is first offered to him. His
association with the fox at the moment of its death is sufficiently startling, whether or not one accepts my metaphorical
interpretation of it, to make us scrutinise the moral and
thematic implications of the time-related events in the bedroom at that moment.

In his eagerness to possess the girdle, Gawain yields to the
Lady's importunities even before she can add her request that
he *disceuer hit neuer*, and readily agrees *þat neuer wyȝe
schulde hit wyt, iwysse, bot þay twayne / for noȝte* (1864–5).
Though he seems entirely unconscious that what he has just
promised *to lelly layne fro hir lorde* he is bound by the
Exchange of Winnings compact to surrender to him that
evening, we must anticipate a conflict of duties compelling the

choice between lack of *cortaysye* towards his hostess or breach of *fela3schyp* with his host which Gawain has skilfully avoided throughout his stay at Hautdesert (Haines (1976), p. 243). True, his commitment to the Lady is informal and social, his compact with her husband a formal one – *'sware with trawpe'* (1108) – in God's name; in any conflict between them, the latter must surely take precedence.[2] The superb tact which has so far helped him to avoid offence to either may still suggest to Gawain some method of surrendering the girdle to Bertilak without betraying the Lady's confidence. But if he has no wish to keep it, the same tact might have allowed him to avoid acceptance or, at least, the promise of concealment: 'we cannot infer (after his displays of skill in extricating himself from similar social traps) that he had no choice but to agree; he agrees to the deception principally because he sees in the belt the possibility of saving his life' (Waldron, p. 17).

Some critics see the moment of acceptance as the central crisis of the poem; yet, though it happens before our eyes, we are hardly more aware of what has occurred than Gawain appears to be (Howard, p. 237). What the poet allows us to see is his estimate of the value of the girdle in the dreaded encounter at the Green Chapel (1855–8), his agreement to conceal it (1863–5), and his hiding of it *per he hit eft fonde* (1875). At the same time, by the language in which he expresses his hero's thoughts, the poet associates him with the thievish fox (see above, p. 72). But is Gawain, at this point, a thief in fact or only in intention? If by the canons of chivalric romance, with its respect for the technicalities of medieval law, the kisses pressed upon Gawain by the Lady properly belong to his host under the terms of the Exchange of Winnings, then the girdle too rightly belongs to Bertilak. The moral theory underlying contemporary law, as expressed by St Thomas Aquinas, left no doubt that retention by concealment constituted theft: '. . . the essence of theft consists in its being the surreptitious taking of somebody else's property. . . . Retaining what one owes another does the same sort of harm as taking something from another, and this is why unjustifiable taking must be held to include unjustifiable retention' (Aquinas, *Summa*: 2a2æ. 66, 3).[3] The principle would be familiar to laymen in the popular manuals intended for their spiritual guidance: 'ȝif þou wyth-holdyst oþeres godys whiche þou owyst to restore, in purpos & in wyll noȝt to ȝeldyn it, it is dedly synne' (*Jacob's Well*, p. 136).[4]

The moral issue is clear, but until Bertilak returns, Gawain's intention to keep or surrender the girdle, and hence his guilt or innocence, cannot be certainly known, though the circumstances in which he accepts it must raise suspicions that the Pentangle Knight is about to break his chivalric code. Meanwhile, the fate of the fox seems out of keeping with Gawain's petty theft, actual or potential – whether or not the flaying of the animal, as well as its thievish nature, is metaphorically associated with him.

There remains, however, the other major variation which distinguishes the day of the fox from those of the deer and boar – Gawain's confession. No element in the poem has given rise to more controversy, not only in relation to its thematic significance, but its sacramental validity, and even its content. The sacramental issue, as defined by Burrow (pp. 106–10), is that the confession could not be a valid one since – in his opinion – Gawain had from the beginning no intention of surrendering the girdle, and could not be absolved from the sin of breaking his obligation to Bertilak while retaining the object wrongfully so acquired. Of those who have disagreed with Burrow, some are convinced of the validity of the confession on the grounds that Gawain's subsequent behaviour reflects an ease of conscience incompatible with abuse of the sacrament (TGD, p. 123), and that retention of the girdle represents a social rather than a formal breach of *trawþe*, since the Exchange of Winnings can be seen as a game rather than a sworn commitment (Foley, pp. 73–6). Others, while agreeing with Burrow that the girdle was not mentioned, reject his idea that the confession was therefore invalid: some on the grounds that, if Gawain did not recognise that retention of the girdle was a sin, it was not necessary matter for confession, since sin involves full understanding and consent on the part of the sinner (Evans, pp. 275–6); others on the assumption that the retention was only a venial sin, since intention to commit a mortal sin would leave Gawain, without further recourse to a priest, still unabsolved at the end of the poem (Field, pp. 259–63).

Though it is difficult to be fair to complex arguments presented in such abbreviated form, many of them seem to me to rely upon special pleading to avoid unwelcome implications in the poem or justify pre-assumptions on its overall interpretation. Can Foley's reading of the Exchange of Winnings be tenable in view of the parallel presentation of the Exchange of Blows as both *layk* and legal compact (see above, pp. 14–15)? Is Field justified in interpreting the confession scene as implying that 'Gawain goes into the chapel intending to keep the belt, and comes out absolved, still intending to keep it' (p. 260) on his judgement of Gawain's spiritual state at the end of the poem? Equally, Howard (pp. 240–1), who argues that, if the priest dissuaded Gawain from active faith in the girdle, he need not then return it and his confession would not be falsified by his failure to do so, and Stevens (p. 77), who suggests that, in the confessional, Gawain may have mentioned the girdle only as the subject of his two conflicting promises to his host and hostess, a venial sin at most, both seem to treat the matter as one of technicalities rather than the moral issue which would concern a priest, his confessant's intention with regard to the property of another. The question of intention is begged still more sharply by Hunt (pp. 4–7) who distinguishes between Gawain's *acceptance* of the girdle, involving only the venial sin of agreeing to the condition of secrecy incompatible with his *trawþe* to Bertilak, and his *concealment* of it from him, a fault which, at the moment of confession, still lies in the future and therefore need not be included: 'until Gawain has committed the sin he cannot very well repent it and be absolved from it' (p. 6).

Clearly, the validity of Gawain's confession and the nature of his fault – if any – are still far from generally agreed; yet these are matters vital to the reading of the poem from this point onwards, and to its thematic interpretation as a whole. I would suggest that approaches to the issue have been somewhat too mechanistic, too much influenced by the concept of the detective story with its correct solution to be determined by the discovery of a number of clues carefully planted by the author. If the poem were constructed on that principle, we might now begin to suspect that modern scholars were more obtuse than medieval readers in arriving at such disparate interpretations, or that the poet was inept in indicating his intentions. But just as few critics could now accept Gollancz's suggestion (p. 123) that the *Gawain*-poet simply failed to notice that his hero had made a sacrilegious confession, it seems equally unlikely that such a meticulous craftsman should have contrived an effect which does not operate coherently – if, perhaps, ambiguously – in the scheme of his poem. It is, to my mind, significant that many of the interpretations given depend upon information derived from later scenes, in particular Gawain's admission of guilt at the Green Chapel, whereas the example of other enigmatic elements suggests that the confession should be meaningful in its immediate context – though its significance may change as the action develops, and appear more highly charged on a second reading. The wooing scenes of Fitt III take on added meaning as part of a complex test of chivalric idealism when their interconnection with the Exchange of Blows contest becomes apparent in Fitt IV; but in their immediate context they are sufficiently identifiable with a traditional romance motif to suggest a test, though not to define its nature and purpose, sufficiently charged with social and emotional tension to imply its importance, and accompanied – if my interpretation of the hunting scenes is correct – with rhetorical parallels sufficiently ominous to warn that its outcome may be grave. Is it not likely that the confession scene is equally, even if not completely, comprehensible in its context, that sufficient evidence has been provided for its immediate interpretation even though it may later take on added significance, and – possibly – that there is rhetorical guidance as to its meaning?

It is my conviction that neither the content nor the validity of Gawain's confession can be determined from the immediate context (1876–84). Like much else in the poem, the scene is presented with so much candour, with such verbal precision, that one is forced to accept the narrative at its face value, whatever doubts may be raised by what precedes and follows it. Critics seem ready to accept that *he asoyled hym surely and sette hym so clene / As domezday schulde haf ben di3t on þe morn* represents the priest's view of the confession as complete and effective (Jacobs, p. 435, n. 7). Since we have no more reason to doubt the poet's sincerity when he tells us that his hero *schrofhym schyrly and schewed his mysdedez, / Of þe more and þe mynne*, should this not represent Gawain's conscious intention in making confession? Imperceptive readers, modern or medieval, may be satisfied by conventional appearances, the ritual purgation of a knight before a dangerous mission. Others may be led to question the efficacy of that purgation by the events which immediately precede it: Gawain's reflection on the value of the girdle to him as *a juel for þe jopardé þat hym iugged were*, his acceptance of it under conditions which threaten to invalidate the Exchange of Winnings compact, and his careful concealment of it where he could find it later. For what purpose? If in order to surrender it to the Lady's husband, why hide it so carefully now? Conceivably, out of concern for the Lady's reputation; such an intimate garment could scarcely be left lying on his bed for the servants to find. If it has merely been put out of sight until the ever-tactful Gawain can find a discreet opportunity to give it to his host, then concealment does not imply intention to retain. If there is no intention to retain it, the girdle need not be concerned in Gawain's confession. True, its surrender will involve breach of his social commitment to the Lady, but that too can consist only in intention not in deed at the moment of the confession. And intention cannot be known from the immediate record of the poem which preserves the secret of the confessional under its impenetrably candid surface.[5]

The contemporary reader would, however, be stimulated to a critical examination of the context by just those enigmatic elements which have led to such divergent modern interpretations (*cf.* Haines (1976), p. 243). The doctrine of penance, with its promise of spiritual purgation for sinful man, was of vital interest to all who hoped for salvation, the subject of theological controversy, of endless sermons aimed at the humble illiterate, and technical manuals fascinating to the educated layman who wished to save his soul. In the early church, penance was a rare sacrament, normally accorded only once in a lifetime after baptism, and involved private confession to a bishop or priest, an ordered course of public humiliation, and a reconciliation or absolution, usually in public. It was, apparently, the duty of the clergy to seek out and obtain confessions from those in sin; spontaneous confession only gradually developed. By the early Middle Ages, a system of penitence developed in the Irish monasteries, and involving private penance and private reconciliation administered by a priest, had spread to most of Western Europe. This system was formalised by the Fourth Lateran Council of 1215, which made annual confession obligatory on all Christians who had reached the age of discretion.[6]

Long before this date, the growing complexity of penitential doctrine prompted the production of manuals for the guidance of confessors in administering it. The earliest identifiable examples of these penitentials were associated with the early Celtic Church, whose influence gave them wide currency in the West. They had, however, no formal authority, and as the Roman Church grew more highly organised it attacked this form of instruction which rendered a priest comparatively independent of his bishop in the administration of penance. But, finding them too useful to suppress, the bishops themselves began to adopt the methods and materials of the penitentials, striving only to restrict their use to the clergy. Though examples in Anglo-Saxon, Old Irish, and Icelandic have survived, they are predominantly in Latin. Yet they reflect the societies in which they were produced, for example by including amongst their penitential provisions elements of secular justice, such as commutation of penalties by money payments graded according to the rank of the person offended against or the nature of the injury inflicted. Despite the purists' disapproval of such commutation, the penitentials exercised a civilising and humanising influence upon church discipline and social morality; without their guidance many parish priests would have been ill fitted for their confessional function.[7] The establishment of obligatory confession by the Fourth Lateran Council, and papal permission to wandering friars to supplement parish priests as confessors, made them still more essential. Vernacular examples multiplied and their content was widened by decrees, such as that of Archbishop Peckham in 1281, that the people were to be instructed four times a year in the principal tenets of the faith, including the Ten Commandments, the Seven Deadly Sins, and the Sacraments, with particular emphasis upon penance. In England, the technical manuals in Latin interpreting Canon Law on such matters were matched by vernacular versions intended for the instruction of laymen, some cast in the form of sermons, some as allegorical treatises; others were complications of *exempla* illustrating the vices and virtues, or brief outlines of the main points of belief in metrical form.[8]

If, as generally assumed, the *Gawain*-poet was also the author of *Pearl*, *Patience* and *Cleanness*, there is no need to doubt the extent of his theological knowledge or the sophistication of technical interest and interpretative ability which he expected in his audience – or some of them at least, since his poems can be read satisfactorily at various levels of thematic penetration. In reading the blandly impenetrable account of Gawain's confession at Hautdesert, even those with only an informed layman's knowledge of penitential doctrine would, I suggest, recognise not one clear-cut implication but a maze of interpretative possibilities. As on the appearance of the Green Knight at Arthur's Court or the Lady's first entrance to Gawain's bedroom (see above, pp. 8–9), the concreteness and apparent candour of the narrative raise a host of queries, stimulated, in those instances, by the intentions – unknown but suspected – of the visitants, and here by Gawain's intention – unknown but suspect – with regard to the girdle. Has he always intended to surrender it to Bertilak? – in which case it need not have been directly concerned in his confession, though the breach of his promise to the Lady seemingly implied should, if regarded as a formal rather than a social commitment, have been admitted as a venial fault. Has he belatedly realised that his original impulse to keep it would be a breach of the Exchange of Winnings compact and confessed his sinful intention? – in which case it will have been a condition of his absolution that he make restitution to Bertilak as the injured party at the earliest opportunity. Has he failed to consider the implications of his acceptance or to realise that any sin was involved in the retention of the girdle, and so made no mention of it in his confession? Or has he realised all the implications and, knowing that admission of sin is incompatible with retention of its fruits, consciously concealed this particular fault from his confessor?

A false confession or one unconsciously incomplete seems

unthinkable in the Pentangle Knight, so scrupulous in chivalric practice, so self-aware in matters of conduct. But at the climax of a sequence in which his self-awareness has been increasingly preoccupied by his own reputation, by concern for his chivalry in the approaching test at the Green Chapel, scrupulosity may have been overwhelmed by the natural human instinct for self-preservation. The poet has already reminded us how vulnerable the highest chivalry can be to instinctive reaction in moments of stress: Arthur, stung by the Green Knight's taunts, seizes his axe and commits the court to the Exchange of Blows compact (316–31); Gawain, covering his embarrassment at the Lady's first entrance to his bedroom, makes the sign of the cross in feigned surprise, seemingly without awareness of misusing a sacred symbol (1195–203). Whether or not the gesture was sacriligious must depend on his motive in making it; the thoughts and actions which precede suggest a conscious intention to deceive (see above, p. 12). If his reflection on the protective value of the girdle and his action in hiding it imply an intention to keep it as a talisman against the Green Knight's axe, a self-protective impulse as instinctive as that of the fox shrinking back from Bertilak's sword, the suspicion that he has abused the sacrament of penance cannot be avoided.

To some critics the suspicion amounts to conviction. Like Gollancz, Engelhardt (p. 222) interprets the confession as manifestly false. Others, whether they accept it as valid or not, see Gawain's intention in making it as the essential issue. There are those to whom his behaviour suggests that he cannot acknowledge any sin in respect of the girdle, even to himself: 'There are moral issues which the rational mind will not face, or face dispassionately, when survival seems to be at stake and when so many mitigating circumstances can be evoked to cloud the issue' (Green, R., pp. 192–3). His moral blindness, Spearing suggests, is due to his habitual concern with his reputation: 'it is precisely his consciousness, his self-awareness or *concience*, that is at fault' (p. 225). For others, this lapse in moral awareness extends to the retention of the girdle itself: 'Face to face one moment with the fear of death, and offered in the next the gift of life, the hero is thoroughly confouded by his warring emotions, and in this confused state nits two grave breaches of the chivalric code' (Shedd,). However confident, such an opinion is based on cx..apolation of the stated facts which, though they imply readiness to take the girdle, do not prove a fixed intention to retain it: 'We are left in no doubt about Gawain's willigness and intention to accept the girdle, but we are left very uncertain about his consciousness of concealing the girdle, which is presented negatively merely as an omission, and nowhere as an intended and deliberate act' (Hunt, p. 14). But to the contemporary reader it is precisely this vagueness as to intention which would waken concern for Gawain, since penitential doctrine lays so much stress upon motivation in and conscious awareness of sin.

The sacramental essence of penance is the relationship between the sinner and his God, in which the priest acts as intermediary: 'For what the penitent sinner does and says signifies that his heart has turned away from sin; likewise the priest, through what he does and says with regard to the penitent, signifies the work of God forgiving sin' (Aquinas, *Summa*: 3a. 84, 1). And the root of that relationship, on the sinner's part, is contrition: 'a sorrow of the soul and a detestation of the sin committed, with a purposing not to sin for the future'.[9] All sin is an offence against God; and the greater the offence to the Creator, the greater should be the repentance: 'Vorþenchinge acseþ grat zorȝe and greate zykinges of herte, uor þet he heþ y-wreþed his sseppere. And þe more þet me him heþ y-wreþed, þe more gratter ssel by þe zorȝe.' (Dan Michel, *Ayenbite*, p. 171.)[10] The gravity of the sin depends upon the degree to which it alienates the sinner from his God: '. . . when the soul is so disordered by sin that it turns away from its ultimate goal, God, to whom it is united by charity, then we speak of mortal sin. However, when this disorder stops short of turning away from God, then the sin is venial' (Aquinas, *Summa*: 1a2æ. 72, 5). The distinction, as educated laymen understood it, is clearly stated in Chaucer's Parson's Tale: 'Soothly, whan man loveth any creature moore than Jhesu Crist oure Creatour, thanne is it deedly synne. And venial synne is it, if man love Jhesu Crist lasse than hym oghte' (X, 357).[11] Both mortal and venial sin, in so far as they involve a turning away from God, represent a failure in faith and

charity, a lessening of that *caritas* which man owes his Creator, or its perversion to lesser ends. The remedy for both lies in repetance, that 'free movement of the will, hating and detesting the sinful act, turning from it to God's mercy with the hope of forgiveness based on faith',[12] whose initial impulse is contrition. Contrition may be perfect or imperfect: in the former case its basis is love of God, in the latter fear of punishment.[13]

In the later Middle Ages, as we shall see (see below, pp. 139–41), the degree of contrition required for effective penance was the subject of debate amongst theologians. Readers of *Sir Gawain*, conscious that fear of death underlies the hero's seeming self-absorption and that he has considered the protective value of the girdle at the Green Chapel, may wonder how he evaluates the sin of withholding it from its rightful owner. The fact that he goes to confession immediately after accepting the girdle need not imply that he is conscious of any sinful intention respecting it. Knights in peril of death had such obvious need of shrift that any priest might hear their confession:

> And of a mon þat schal go fyȝte
> In a bateyl for hys ryȝte,
> Hys schryft also þou myȝte here,
> Þaȝ he þy pareschen neuer were
> (Mirk, *Instructions*, 739–42)[14]

We cannot follow Gawain into the confessional, but we know what was required of him if he had any mortal sin on his conscience: '. . . pardon for mortal sin calls for a more explicit repentance, namely that a person actually detests the mortal sin committed as much as he can. This means that he strives to remember every one of his mortal sins, so as to reject each in particular. This, however, is not necessary for the forgiveness of venial sin' (Aquinas, *Summa*: 3a. 87, 1). Such premeditation is an essential aspect of contrition:

. . . a-forn þi schryfte þou muste haue a-forn-recordyng, a-forn-rehersyng, a-for-syȝt, a-forn-stodying, a-forn-avysement, þat þou mowe knowe þi synnes in þi mynde, þat afterward in þi schryfte þou fayle noȝt thruȝ forȝetynge.
(*Jacob's Well*, I, p. 179)[15]

We may wonder whether the rapidity with which he passes

from concealing the girdle to entering the chapel in the next line has allowed Gawain to weigh his motives and consider whether there is anything sinful in them. But we must assume that one who has elsewhere shown himself so conscientious in his religious duties knows what is required of him in confession: first contrition, *sorowe in our herte that we hafe synnede*, then *opyn scrifte of mouthe how we hafe synnede.*[16] And we can anticipate the questions which, according to Myrc, the priest was instructed to ask, some of them painfully apposite to matters which may be on Gawain's conscience:

> Hast þow falsly be for-swore
> For any þyng þow couetest zore?
> Hast þow I-gete any thynge
> Wyth false countenans and glosynge?
>
> (Mirk, *Instructions*, 1191–4)

Not least the reminder of the essential nature of mortal sin:

> Hast þou worschypet any þynge
> More þen god, oure heuene kynge?
>
> (Mirk, *Instructions*, 853–4)

How will Gawain answer such questions?

The seal of the confessional justifies the poet's silence on the subject, but the immediate juxtaposing of potential crime and confession, and some suspicious elements in Gawain's behaviour after absolution, stimulate us to penetrate it in imagination. As in the case of Gawain's judgement on the Green Knight's challenge to the Round Table and its outcome (see above, pp. 12–15), we seek motive and intention behind the impenetrably candid narrative. For the contemporary layman reasonably informed on the doctrine of penance, the circumstances would suggest many possible interpretations. Guided by the bland surface of the confession scene, one might suppose that Gawain, having accepted the girdle only to escape the Lady's importunities, had from the first intended to surrender it to Bertilak as his due, and so has no sinful intention regarding it. His concealment of it might then appear as a characteristically tactful act to protect the Lady's reputation from scandal pending an equally tactful presentation to her husband, in which his skill in courtly conversation may conceal its origin as effectually as it has so far concealed the source of the surrendered kisses. If that should not avoid a breach of his undertaking to the Lady, he would be guilty of a social fault or, at most, a venial sin (Hunt, p. 6) to be included in his general confession on this or a later occasion.

Alternatively, we might suppose that, having initially taken the girdle with the intention of keeping it, Gawain immediately afterwards realised the implications of retaining what properly belongs to Bertilak. Such an act, if done openly, is robbery; if in secret, theft (Aquinas, *Summa*: 2a2ae. 61, 3):

> ... pryve thefte; þat is, whann þou takyst ony thyng priuely þat is nouȝt þin, & priuely heldyst it as þin owyn, and ȝit þou art holdyn a trewe man, but þou art a prevy theef. *(Jacob's Well*, p. 128)

But if Gawain himself has realised the sin inherent in his initial acceptance, the secrecy implied by his concealment of the girdle may be a sign of moral awakening: 'When returning something would appear gravely harmful to the person concerned or to others, it should not be done then and there, for restitution is for the benefit of the receiver, ... [The taker] should keep it in order to return it at a fitting time or should hand it over to another for safer keeping' (Aquinas, *Summa*: 2a2æ. 62, 5). Despite our suspicions, concealment may be the first step in restitution; in which case there will be no theft to confess.

If, however, concealment implies intention to retain, Gawain is already in sin: 'Because it is an evil a sin can be fully a sin at any one point, ... Hence a sin committed simply interiorly is one species of sin' (Aquinas, *Summa*: 3a. 90, 3).[17] 'ȝif þou coueyte an-oþerys good, wyth full wyll for to haue it, ȝif þou myȝt, vnryȝtfully, it is dedly synne, þouȝ þou neuere haue it, for þin euyl wyll' *(Jacob's Well*, p. 135). Were he to be reminded by his confessor:

> Þow myȝte synge als sore in þoght,
> As þou þat dede hadest I-wroght
> (Mirk, *Instructions*, 965–6)

how would Gawain answer his enquiry:

> Hast þou, by maystry or by craft,
> Any mon hys good be-raft?
> (Mirk, *Instructions*, 939–40)

And if he were shocked into recognising and confessing his fault, how would the priest view it? His catechism should seek not merely the material circumstances but the underlying motives which constitute the nature of the sin. His evaluation must consider the lack of *caritas* involved: '. . . charity consists primarily in loving God, and, secondly, in loving our neighbour which includes wishing him well and acting accordingly. Stealing, however, damages one's neighbour through his property . . . Theft is, therefore, a mortal sin in so far as it is contrary to charity' (Aquinas, *Summa*: 2a2æ. 66, 6). But it will also consider the purpose for which the theft has been committed:

> The difference between a mortal and a venial sin . . . amounts to the difference between a sin committed out of malice and a sin committed out of frailty or inadvertance.
>
> (Aquinas, *Summa*: 1a2æ. 88, 2)
>
> One who sins venially embraces a temporal good not by way of seeking fulfilment in it as end, but by way of making use of it under his abiding, though not actual, intention of God.
>
> (Aquinas, *Summa*: 1a2æ. 88, 1)

On the assumption, which seems a reasonable one, that theft of the girdle would not be an intrinsically mortal sin, such factors would enter into any judgement as to the nature of the fault; but since we lack information on these matters, we cannot know what a confessor's judgement would be. We may, however, note some mitigating factors. Gawain's taking of the girdle may be justified by necessity:

> If, however, there is so urgent and blatant a necessity that the immediate needs must be met out of whatever is available, as when a person is in imminent danger and he cannot be helped in any other way, then a person may legitimately supply his own needs out of another's property, whether he does so secretly or flagrantly. And in such a case there is strictly speaking no theft or robbery.
>
> (Aquinas, *Summa*: 2a2æ. 66, 7)[18]

This provision, however, properly refers to material necessity; yet it raises the issue of Gawain's need, the alternatives open to him in the face of impending death, and the dubious status of the girdle as a solution to his dilemma. Similarly, the provision concerning petty thefts – 'ʒif it be but a lytel harm, as an appyl or swich an-oþer smal thyng þat þou wost wel it schal noʒt dysplese þi neyʒboure, þowʒ he wyst it, þan it is

venyal synne' (*Jacob's Well*, p. 137)[19] – provokes consideration of the value which Gawain places upon the girdle as
talisman, and the significance which Bertilak might attribute
to it as love-token (*drurye*). Whether or not, in the light of all
the circumstances, the priest would judge Gawain's intention
to constitute mortal or venial sin, his absolution will presuppose a radical change of heart: 'Just as a mortal sin cannot be
pardoned as long as the will clings to the sin, so neither can a
venial sin; while the cause remains, so does the effect'
(Aquinas, *Summa*: 3a. 87, 1). It will be conditional upon
restitution of the girdle to its rightful owner (Aquinas,
Summa: 2a2æ. 62, 2), and the priest himself may offer to
provide a discreet channel for its restoration (Aquinas,
Summa: 2a2æ. 62, 6). So Gawain may leave the chapel
already purged of all sin by contrition, confession, and restitution.

There is, however, a fourth interpretation of the confession
scene which gives a sinister significance to its candid surface.
If Gawain's concealment of the girdle indicates an intention
to keep it which he has not consciously realised, he may be
incapable of the act of violition necessary for penitence:
'. . . penitence, as a virtue, is seated in the will. And its proper
act is a purpose of amendment for deeds committed against
God. . . . penitence is not in the memory, but does presuppose
it' (Aquinas, *Summa*: 3a. 85, 4). A failure of memory on
Gawain's part seems improbable; not to recollect a theft so
recently committed would be to show a laxness in the examination of conscience before confession which would be itself
sinful, a species of Sloth: 'Efter sleauþe is uoryetinge. Vor
huo þet ys sleauuol ofte uoryet. Vor þise tuo zennes of
uoryetynge, hit yualþ ofte þet he ne can him ssriue' (Dan
Michel, *Ayenbite*, p. 32).[20] If Gawain were unconscious of sin
because of spiritual sloth he would be in peril of damnation:

> Some men, whan here synne ys wroȝt,
> Hyt no more cumþ yn here þoȝt,
> And ȝyueþ no fors, þat he forȝeteþ
> Hys synne; and hym þe fend eteþ.
> (Mannyng, *Handlyng Synne*, 10829–32)

If, on the other hand, he is genuinely unconscious of any sinful intention in respect of the girdle, his spiritual state must depend on the degree of culpability involved in his ignorance:

Since all sin is voluntary, ignorance diminishes sin only in so far as it lessens free will, and if it does not lessen freedom it does not lessen sin. Quite clearly, when ignorance totally excuses from sin because it is completely involuntary, sin is not only diminished but eliminated. When ignorance accompanies sin but does not cause it, sin is neither eliminated nor diminished. Ignorance diminishes sin only when it is a cause of sin but does not entirely excuse one from sin.

(Aquinas, *Summa*: 1a2æ. 76, 4)

Can the Pentangle Knight, so socially and spiritually scrupulous, be ignorant that, by the Exchange of Winnings agreement, the girdle belongs to Sir Bertilak, and that to withhold it from him without due cause is theft? If not, can he be free from sin, unless unaware of any malign intention in his concealment of the girdle, improbable though that may seem?

And what can be his spiritual state if, fully conscious of a resolve to retain the girdle, he has concealed his theft from the priest, or confessed it with no intention of desisting from it? To hide a sin by neglect of confession is opposed to penance (Aquinas, *Summa*: 3a. 84, 6), and to persist in it despite confession is to make a mockery of the sacrament: 'For a man is a mocker and not penitent who, while doing penance at the same time does what he repents having done, in that he intends to do again what he did before, or even actually commits the same or another kind of sin' (Aquinas, *Summa*: 3a. 84, 10). Consequently, the confession as a whole will be invalid, since 'one cannot be truly penitent who repents of one sin, but not of another' (Aquinas, *Summa*: 3a. 86, 3). And if Gawain has consciously rejected the sacrament, to his unabsolved sin will be added the sin of ingratitude:

The ingratitude of a sinner is sometimes a specific sin, sometimes not, but rather it is a circumstance generally consequent upon every mortal sin as this is committed against God. For sin receives its species from the intention of the sinner . . . If, then, any sinner commits some sin out of contempt for God or a gift received, his sin takes on the species of ingratitude.

(Aquinas, *Summa*: 3a. 88, 4)

Assuming that his turning away from God for the sake of the girdle constitutes a mortal sin, Gawain, by choosing to remain in sin, is doubly a thief:

Þe zeneȝere is godes þief, uor þe guodes of his lhorde þet ne byeþ him bote ylend uor to wynne. Þet byeþ þe guodes of kende and of grace and of hap, heurof him behoueþ rekeninge and scele yelde wel straytliche. He hise heþ folliche y-spended ine euele wones and al ylayd to an hazard.

(Dan Michel, Ayenbite, p. 171)

His motive for rejecting the divine gift of grace is hidden in Gawain's heart, but the various alternatives are all equally ominous. He may be motivated by that species of pride which leads a man to fear the world's opinion more than God and so hide his sins out of shame: 'And in þi schryfte, whanne þou for schame helyst ony foul synne, or in colouryng þi synne in schryfte, ony parcell to o preest & an-oþer parcell to an-oþer preest; all þis is ypocrysie' (*Jacob's Well*, p. 74). Or by that species which leads him to sin more boldly from over-confidence in God's readiness to forgive: '... þis cornere of pride, þat is boldnes, is fals renayinge, which is in foure. On is, whan þou forsakyst þi god, & takyst þe to þe feend. Anoþer is, whanne þou forsakyst & holdyst noȝt þi truthe' (*Jacob's Well*, p. 73). The breach of troth with God which such apostasy involves is interpreted by contemporary commentators in feudal terms:

Þe þridde ontreuþe þet comþ of prede ys renayrie. He ys wel renay þet, þet land þet he halt of his lhorde, deþ in-to þe hond of his uyende and deþ him manhode. Zuych zenne makeþ ech þet zeneȝeþ dyadliche, uor þanne alzo moche ase of him is he deþ manhode to þe dyeule, and becomþ his þrel, and him yelt al þet he halt of god and bodi and zaule, and oþre guodes, þet he deþ to þe seruice of þe dyeule.

(Dan Michel, Ayenbite, p. 19)

The sinner in deadly sin is seen as a traitor to God:

... he is godes bezuykere [*MED biswikere* n. 'Traitor'], uor þe castel of his herte and of his bodye, þet god him heþ ytake to loki, he heþ yolde to his yuo dyadlich, þet is þe dyeuel.

(Dan Michel, Ayenbite, p. 171)

Þe ferthe fote brede of wose in coueytise is tresoun; þat is, whan þou art fals to hym þat þou schuldyst be trewe to, for coueytise, as Judas, whan he solde crist for xxx d. as a fals traytoure, Mat. xxvj. ... Ryȝt so, whanne þou art lying, or falsly sweryng, or in ony oþer fraude dysseyvyng þi broþer for ony wynnyng, or dost ony falsnes or wrong, or heldyst aȝens trewthe, þou dost tresoun, & sellyst trewthe, þat is, crist.

(Jacob's Well, p. 122)

If he chooses to remain in sin because he doubts the power of redemption, he breaks one of the fundamental conditions for penance: '. . . that a man be nat despeired of the mercy of Jhesu Crist, as Caym or Judas' (Chaucer, Parson's Tale, X, 1015).

Neither the language of treason nor the examples of Cain and Judas as archetypal traitors are surprising in a penitential context. It was entirely natural for medieval writers to interpret the sacramental relationship between God and man in terms of the fundamental bond of feudal society, the struggle between good and evil as a perpetual war in which those who yielded to sin surrendered to the Enemy their God-given souls, and sinners who in arrogant self-confidence rejected the offer of divine grace or in abject self-contempt despaired of redemption as rebels in breach of their *trawþe*. The sacrament of penance is the means by which the Devil in a man's heart is brought to a traitor's death:

His heaued is i hacked of, 7 he is i sleien oðe monne, so sone so he euer is riht sori uor his sunnen, 7 haueð schrifte on heorte.

(Ancrene Riwle, p. 135)

To reject or abuse it is to ally oneself with him and those who do his work: Cain, Herod, Caiaphas, Julian the Apostate, and Judas, all treated in medieval literature as traitors to God.[21] Their crime is spiritual treason and, where it would not conflict with biblical record, the medieval imagination condemned them to the most ignominious form of the traitor's death, flayed alive as Caiaphas was, *In tokne of tresoun & trey þat he wroзt*, by Titus and Vespasian, or after death, as Julian was by the Persian king Sapor. The archetype of spiritual treason, Judas, whose name is synonymous with 'traitor' (*MED Judas*, n. 1(*a*)), died by his own hand, despairing of God's grace. His despair was itself a sin, the climax of a complex of ingratitude, betrayal, hypocrisy, and theft:

He mad hyme his procuratore,
Þo he wyste he suld be traytore;
For quhat thing euir gyffyne was
To Criste, vthyre mare or lese,
Cryste gefit hyme ay in зemsele,
Þo he was thefe 7 ay wald steyle.

(Legends of the Saints, XII, 241–6)

When, as Gawain considers the value of the girdle to him under threat of death, his thoughts are cast in the devious language of the fox-hunt (see above, p. 72), the reader may assume that he is being associated with the thievish nature of the fox. But the symbolism which medieval writers based upon the natural wiliness of the beast was complex, breeding many moral distinctions out of the deceit which it used to satisfy its greed. Amongst the seven deadly sins, it typifies Covetousness:

þe vox of ȝiscunge haueð þeos hweolpes: tricherie, 7 gile, þeofðe, reflac, wite, 7 herrure strenðe, uals-witnesse oðder oð, simonie, gauel, oker, uestschipe of ȝeoue oþer of lone, monsleiht oðerhule. Þeos unþeawes beoð to uoxe uor monie reisuns i efnede; two ich chulle siggen. Muche gile is iðe voxe, 7 so is ine ȝiscunge of worldliche biȝeate.
(*Ancrene Riwle*, p. 90)

Gawain may well covet the girdle as *a juel for þe jopardé*, but in all such desires there are three degrees:

Þe uorme is cogitaciun, þe oðer is affectiun, þe þridde is kunsence.
(*Ancrene Riwle*, p. 129)

If his action when he *Hid hit ful holdely* signifies consent, a yielding to his desires, contemporary readers might well suspect him of imitating the fox in other moral failings than *þeofðe*: breach of undertaking to the Lady or to her husband, depending on whether he ultimately surrenders the girdle or not; betrayal of his feudal obligation to either host or hostess. But readers striving to reconcile Gawain's apparent intention of theft with the asserted completeness of his confession would be led to consider another form of *tricherie*, that abuse of the sacrament of which Henryson accused the *wylie tratour Tod*.[22] And without, at this stage, being able to do more than guess at the moral motive for such abuse on Gawain's part, they might well be made uneasy by his association with the fox, so often in contemporary tradition a symbol of deceit, pride, and hypocrisy, and the type of Satan.[23]

If the ambiguity of the confession scene gives these symbolic attributes of the fox disturbing relevance to Gawain, they in turn add ominous meaning to the metaphorical significance of the beast's death: that shrinking from fear of physical death, the knight has fallen into a host of moral errors as into the mouths of hell-hounds which threaten the death of the soul. The ambiguous characterisation of Bertilak allows him to be seen as the Devil hunting souls or as an agent of divine retribution. The echoes of the hue and cry raised by his questing hounds may suggest due process for the punishment of material theft, but also, metaphorically, that incurred for the spiritual theft involved in abusing the divine gift of grace (see above, pp. 98–9). If the flaying in which it ends is seen as a traitor's death, it may imply the spiritual treason of a Judas motivated by pride or by despair. That it is a death of the soul which threatens is ironically hinted by the clamour raised over the dying beast, *Pe rich rurd pat per watz raysed for Renaude saule* (1916).

To the modern mind such an interpretation may seem laboured and mechanistic; to the medieval reader, accustomed to read even secular narrative at more than one level of meaning, the association of ideas would be more instinctive, guided by the multiple, inter-related forms of the metaphorical hunt. The significance of the flaying of the fox is shocking, its realisation abrupt; but the effect is characteristic of the poem, no more abrupt than the realisation that the outcome of the Exchange of Blows test depended upon the Exchange of Winnings game, no more startling in implication than the survival of the headless Green Knight or the realisation that Sir Bertilak and he are one. The poet cannot be accused of misleading the reader by false clues in any of these instances; he has merely manipulated romance tradition in unconventional ways. In this instance, having twice suggested through the metaphorical hunt a possible course of conduct for Gawain in the parallel wooing scenes and twice disappointed expectation, the triple patterns of folk-tale justify him in fulfilling expectation on the third occasion. If he intended the *asay* and dismemberment of the deer and boar to imply the form of trial and execution deserved by Gawain should he yield to the Lady's amorous temptation and commit sexual treason, it is reasonable to expect a related significance in the flaying of the fox on a day when we suspect Gawain of imitating its thievish behaviour in yielding to the moral temptation represented by her girdle. But on the third day, as on the other two, though the metaphorical relationship implies various narrative possibilities, it does not dictate the narrative outcome. The fate of the fox may be interpreted as the feudal penalty for sexual treason incurred on the aggravated evidence of the girdle, should it be surrendered to Bertilak; or, should it be permanently withheld, as a metaphor for the death of the soul which knowingly rejects the divine gift of grace. Whether Gawain is guilty of any breach of *trawþe*, feudal or spiritual, of treason to man or God, must depend on the outcome of the Exchange of Winnings. Anticipation of further variations in the daily pattern of events creates a tension which is both narrative and thematic.

One such variation is implicit in the confession scene. For Bertilak, each day's hunting is preceded by attendance at mass (1135, 1414, 1690); on the first two days Gawain also attends mass before he eats (1311, 1558), but not on this occasion. If his confession was followed by communion we are not told so. It may seem so much a matter of routine as not to warrant mention (Burrow, p. 117); or, if we doubt the validity of his confession, the omission may appear highly suspicious, 'another indication of Gawain's current "untruth"' (Burrow, p. 118). To receive communion in a state of sin is itself a form of spiritual high treason: '. . . those [sins] which you have committed in secret, of such make confession secretly to your priests before you approach the Body of the Lord, because he who receives unworthily, will with Judas be guilty of the death of the Lord.'[24] If Gawain has knowingly abused both sacraments, then the doom which, the poet obliquely reminds us after his confession (1884), may await him tomorrow at the Green Chapel, will also bring the doomsday of his soul.

Yet he passes the remainder of this third day with such seeming enjoyment that everyone comments: '*Þus myry he watz neuer are, / Syn he com hider*'. The poet stimulates us to consider the cause of such lightheartedness by bland comments on Gawain's pleasure in the company of *both* the ladies, repeated as the hunters return to court (1924–7), when, in the light of the fox's death, their irony may be more apparent: *Among þe ladies for luf he ladde much ioye*. The linking of the two ladies as before (see above, pp. 9–10) reminds us that the identity of the hostess, her relationship to her óminous *alter ego*, and the motive for her wooing still remain obscure. So does its success or failure. Since she has had no amorous success with Gawain, what *luf* now gladdens him? Gratitude for her gift of a potent talisman? Self-love confident in its protective power? Neither suggests the surrender of the girdle required by a valid confession consistent with Christian *caritas*, that love which binds man to man, and man to God. In either case, if Gawain's *ioye* is heartfelt, it implies moral blindness; if feigned, at best social tact, at worst cynical hypocrisy covering conscious wrong-doing.[25]

We may expect these ambiguities to be resolved by the third and final repetition of the Exchange of Winnings (1928–51). But it too is marked by variations from the daily pattern and consequent ironies. For the first time Gawain's dress is mentioned – blue silk and ermine; blue and white are the colours of the Virgin (Blanch, p. 81; Gallant, p. 48), blue the colour of fidelity (Burrow, pp. 111–12). But if Mary's knight has preserved his chastity in the wooing, can he now maintain his fidelity both to the Lady and to her husband, or has he already broken his *trawþe* to God? In another variation, he forestalls Bertilak in the exchange, pressing the three kisses upon him *al with gomen*. It is for the reader to interpret his haste: the readiness of an easy conscience; the embarrassed *empressement* of one conscious of cheating in a game, but nothing more (Evans, p. 727); the boldness of a shameless hypocrite? – in which case the kisses may evoke associations with the hypocrisy of Judas at Gethsemane.

As on previous occasions, the kisses raise jokes as to their value:

> 'Bi Kryst,' quoþ þat oþer knyʒt, 'ʒe cach much sele
> In cheuisaunce of þis chaffer, ʒif ʒe hade goud chepez.'
> 'ʒe, of þe chepe no charg,' quoþ chefly þat oþer,
> 'As is pertly payed þe chepez þat I aʒte.'   (1938–41)

All the ironies of the earlier exchange scenes (see above, pp. 51–3 and pp. 62–3) – the implication that though the value of Bertilak's kill is manifest that of Gawain's prize depends upon where it was obtained and what significance is attached to it, the association of the material value of the goods with the personal worth (*prys*) of the donor, the intrusion of the

language of commerce into a chivalric game – are sharpened
here by our awareness that they relate to the girdle as well as
the kisses. What value can be attached to a talisman for whose
powers we have only the word of the ambiguous Lady? What
faith does Gawain have in it? What sacrifice of *prys*, of his
identity as the Pentangle Knight, has he made to possess it?
And if he is regardless of the price he has paid for it (*'of þe
chepe no charg'*), can he have forgotten: 'For what shall it
profit a man, if he shall gain the whole world, and lose his own
soul?' (Mark, VIII, 36)? The questions must persist since we
cannot be sure that his claim that what he has obtained has
been *pertly payed* is a lie; the girdle may already have been
surrendered to the priest in the confessional. If it has not
been, and if the object for which it should now be exchanged
(*'þis foule fox felle'*) indicates the price which Gawain has
paid for the girdle, his soul may already be doomed (*'—þe
fende haf þe godez!'*). *'Inoȝ,' quoþ Sir Gawayn*, ending the
Exchange of Winnings – commandingly or with uneasy relief?
The kisses alone have brought no charge of sexual treason;
the girdle has not been surrendered and the suspicion of
spiritual treason is stronger than before. The grounds for that
suspicion are revived as Bertilak recounts *how þe fox watz
slayn*; yet superficially the tension of the Exchange evaporates in hunter's tales.

The company relaxes in the familiar merrymaking of the
evening (1952–9), but there are undertones of excess and
ambiguity: *Gawayn and þe godemon so glad were þay boþe* –
raising the issue of whether their pleasure has a common
source and is equally unfeigned on both sides. At this point on
previous evenings, the lord has taken Gawain apart, to the
chimney-corner in a private chamber (1029–31; 1402;
1664–7) to propose or renew the Exchange of Winnings
compact. The moment seems right for the final fulfilment of
its terms, the surrender of the girdle; but instead Gawain
approaches Bertilak before the whole court, takes leave of
him and reminds him of his promise to provide a guide to the
Green Chapel (1960–76). Though in return he renews his
vow of service to his host (*'I ȝef yow me for on of yourez'*),
whose response – *'Al þat euer I yow hyȝt halde schale I redé'* –
has a double irony: as one who has kept his part of the

compact to one who has not; and, if we suspect his association with the Green Knight, may be expected to keep his part of that other compact which weighs on Gawain's mind ('*þe dome of my wyrdes*'), and against which he has so far retained the girdle. If he has any intention of returning it, this is scarcely the tactful moment; but has he deliberately avoided the privacy of the chimney-corner? Instead, he says farewell to the two ladies *With care and wyth kyssyng* and *Pay bikende hym to Kryst* – with what degree of sincerity on either side? – thanks all the household for their service, and is conducted with the usual ceremony to his bed (1977–90). The example of the Christmas guests who took leave the night before their departure (1126–32) suggests that he will not see his hosts again; and the girdle has not been returned.

> 3if he ne slepe soundyly say ne dar I,
> For he hade muche on þe morn to mynne, 3if he wolde,
>   in þo3t.   (1991–3)

But if he is confident in the possession of his talisman, what has he to fear on the morrow? Yet *ful lyttel he slepes*, while the sounds of the *werbelande wynde* outside (1998–2008) remind us of his winter journey when the knight was exposed to forces of Nature *þat snayped þe wylde*. Whether it is fear of the real world without or a conscience uneasy over his behaviour in the closed world of Hautdesert that keeps him from sleeping, he lies with his eyes discreetly closed, though there is no one to observe his tact.[26] But does discretion cloak ignorance or suppressed awareness? *Bi vch kok þat crue he knwe wel þe steuen*: the voice of the cock may mean no more to Gawain than a reminder of the passing night (Cawley, p. 126), or it may be a warning of what the day will bring, 'a date fixed for a meeting or payment' (*OED steven* n. 2, 2); and to us, perhaps, a reminder of Peter who denied his Lord.

Rising before dawn, Gawain calls for his armour and a chamberlain arms him in all his panoply, scoured free of the rust of his journey from Camelot (2009–24). The scene is a brief, pallid counterpart to the arming ceremony there, reviving all its chivalric and symbolic significances (see above, pp. 17–18), but in such altered circumstances that we may wonder whether *al watz fresch as vpon fyrst* can be applied to the knight as well as to his equipment, or whether the conventional tag *þe gayest into Grece* refers only to the outer man. If this refurbished image of the knight in shining armour seems incompatible with the idea of the green girdle dishonestly retained, it might suggest that now is the moment to confide it discreetly to the chamberlain, if necessary 'under plain cover'. If for surrender to Bertilak, only Gawain's social commitment to the Lady will have been breached, and now, at least, no compromising enquiries can be made; if for return to the Lady, then a momentary impulse has been reconsidered in tranquility, there was no abiding intention to take the girdle, no abuse of the sacraments, no spiritual treason. Instead, Gawain calls for his horse.

But there is a pendant to this arming scene as to the first (2025–42). Behind it, unnamed, hovers the pentangle whose values it ironically evokes: *þe conysaunce of þe clere werkes* suggesting both the fine workmanship with which it has been embroidered on Gawain's surcoat and the pure deeds of chivalry which it symbolises (*cf.* 631, Waldron, p. 116), while the *vertuus stonez* inlaid upon it suggest both the chivalric virtues it represents and the potency of its protective power (Barron, p. 177). The fact that the pentangle is not named is, perhaps, the poet's deliberately self-conscious way of stimulating the reader to recall the *conysaunce* and its complex significance at a moment when Gawain appears to have forgotten them. Christian chivalry, it seems, is no longer an adequate guide and talisman for him:

> ȝet laft he not þe lace, þe ladiez gifte,
> Þat forgat not Gawayn for gode of hymseluen.
> Bi he hade belted þe bronde vpon his balȝe haunchez,
> Þenn dressed he his drurye double hym aboute,
> (2030–3)

The narrative shock, at least to those conscious of the implications of retention of the girdle for the validity of Gawain's confession, is too profound to allow for symbolic itemisation. Instead, the visual impression of the green of the girdle upon the red of the surcoat, the symbolic implications of the physical characteristics of pentangle and lace (endlessness–incom-

pleteness, knotlessness–knottedness, rigidity–pliability, pro-
tected area–trap (Hieatt, p. 121)), the ironic unsuitability of
drurye applied to an emblem of self-love juxtaposed with one
of *afyaunce* in God and *fela3schyp* to fellow-man all create a
contrast of opposites. The contrast implies that if the pentangle symbolises *trawþe*, the girdle must symbolise *vntrawþe*
(Green, p. 192; Hieatt, p. 121). But where the pentangle's
complex terms of reference have been elaborately detailed,
those of the girdle depend upon the reader's interpretation of
the narrative: breach of feudal troth with his host in retaining
his property; breach of the spiritual troth which unites sinful
man to a forgiving God by abusing the sacrament of forgiveness; breach of the unbroken pentangle by putting faith in a
talisman of unknown validity instead of his Christian and
chivalric code? Yet the girdle is not superimposed upon the
pentangle; the two emblems are juxtaposed, as though
Gawain saw no conflict between the values they represent
and assumed that the one was as much *for gode of hymseluen*
as the other. He values the girdle, the poet unnecessarily
insists, not for its material richness:

> Bot for to sauen hymself, when suffer hym byhoued,
> To byde bale withoute debate of bronde hym to were
>   oþer knyffe.   (2040–2)

But the ambiguous vocabulary (*sauen*, *suffer*, *bale* ('the torments (of hell)' – *MED bale* n. 1, 4) questions the worth of a
talisman which, while it may save the body, exposes the soul
to the risk of eternal damnation.

So Gawain sets out to meet the Green Knight already
wearing his green livery, no longer wholly his own man. If he
credits its protective power, he shows no shame in wearing
openly a magical object forbidden to knights in single combat
by the law of arms (Gross, pp. 154–5). To use a protective
charm in an unequal contest against a manifestly supernatural
adversary is a natural human precaution, but also a breach of
chivalry unworthy of the perfectionist aspirations of the Pentangle Knight. We cannot know what faith he puts in it, but
the appearances are bad.[27] Equally, we cannot tell whether he
is conscious of any breach of feudal contract in retaining the
girdle, of any moral breach in the incompatibility between

retention and a valid confession, but the very openness with
which he wears it suggests his moral blindness. As a result, the
concern which we feel for him as he sets out for the Green
Chapel must operate at many levels. In so far as his pentangle
is emblematic of justice, his failure to render his adversary his
just due under the Exchange of Winnings may suggest that he
no longer observes that aspect of his code, and will resort to
some similar duplicity to escape his obligation under the
Exchange of Blows compact.[28] If we suspect that in yielding to
a carnal temptation in order to protect his body from death he
has also fallen prey to spiritual temptation, we may fear that
he has laid himself open not only to human justice as a thief,
but also to divine justice as one guilty of covetousness.[29] The
extreme forms of human justice with which he has been
threatened throughout Fitt III for a breach of *trawþe* with
man imply the inexpressible horror of the penalty incurred by
breach of *trawþe* with God. Divine justice, however, offers
through penance, an escape from such retribution:

. . . redress for an offence takes place in a different way in Penance and in
retributive justice. For in retributive justice redress follows the decision of a
judge, not the will of the offender or the one offended. In Penance,
however, the scales are righted in accord with the will of the sinner and the
judgement of God against whom he sinned. For here not only is the
restoration of the balance of justice sought, as in retributive justice, but
above all reconciliation in friendship. This takes place when the offender
makes amends to suit the good pleasure of the one offended.

(Aquinas, *Summa*: 3a. 90, 2)

If, failing restitution, Gawain has not satisfied the requirements of divine justice, then the mortal chase which
threatened a fatal outcome to the Lady's amorous pursuit of
the knight may seem to be fusing with a form of the sacred
chase in which a divinity pursues aberrant man to reclaim or
destroy him.[30] What awaits Gawain at the Green Chapel:
human justice or divine, the death of the body or the death of
the soul?

NOTES

1 It is significant that Hans Käsmann (p. 137), having established
numerological patterns in Fitt III which suggest a significant and changing

relationship between the hunting and wooing scenes on the first two days, can find no similar principle in the account of the third day – which was, perhaps, the poet's intention.

2   Brian Blakey ('Truth and Falsehood in the *Tristran* of Béroul' in *History and Structure of French* (ed. Barnett *et al.*), Oxford, 1972, pp. 19–29) has pointed out the extreme importance attached to the sworn word in medieval society: 'Perjury was universally abhorred, because it involved a denial of God, which was the ultimate blasphemy; private lying was socially admissable, especially if the individual felt in any way constrained to lie. The combination of these two factors, the individual's tendency to lie and the general abhorrence of perjury, conferred upon the oath a peculiar importance in medieval society, both as a formal judicial procedure and also as a spontaneous indication of personal veracity' (p. 29).

3   Quotations from the *Summa Theologiæ* of St Thomas Aquinas are from the edition and translation by members of the Dominican Order, 60 vols., London, 1964–76.

4   *Jacob's Well: An Englisht Treatise on the Cleansing of Man's Conscience*, ed. A. Brandeis, EETS 115, London, 1900.

5   'We know nothing of Gawain's intentions and there is no firm reason for supposing that he sees that the possession of the girdle involves a sin and persists in wrongful intent' (Hunt, p. 6).

6   On the general history of the sacrament, see O. D. Watkins, *A History of Penance*, New York, 1961. My grateful thanks are due to my colleague Dr D. P. Henry for guiding me through the complexities of penitential doctrine. An excellent outline of the development of penitential doctrine after 1215, its widespread teaching, the vernacular texts in which such teaching reached laymen, and its fundamental influence on a popular literary form is given in Eleanor Prosser's *Drama and Religion in the English Mystery Plays*, Stanford, Cal., 1961, pp. 19–42.

7   On the formal penitentials, see J. T. McNeill and H. M. Gamer, *Medieval Handbooks of Penance*, New York, 1965.

8   See, H. G. Pfander, 'Some Medieval Manuals of Religious Instruction in England and Observations on Chaucer's Parson's Tale', *JEGP*, XXXV (1936), pp. 243–58.

9   As defined by the Council of Trent; cited in *A Catholic Dictionary of Theology*, London, 1962– , s.v. Contrition, p. 122.

10   *Dan Michel's Ayenbite of Inwyt*, ed. R. Morris, EETS 23, London, 1866.

11   *The Works of Geoffrey Chaucer*, ed. F. N. Robinson, 2nd ed., London, 1957.

12   *Catholic Dictionary*, s.v. Contrition, p. 122.

13   See *Ibid.*, p. 123.

14   John Mirk, *Instructions for Parish Priests*, ed. G. Kristensson (Lund Studies in English, 49), Lund, 1974.

15   See also p. 170, and *Robert [Mannyng] of Brunne's Handlyng Synne*, ed. F. J. Furnivall, EETS 119, 123, London, 1901, ll. 10815–40, *Dan Michel's Ayenbite of Inwyt, edn. cit.*, pp. 172–3. The insistence of the

vernacular manuals on the conscious and detailed recollection of sins is significant. The procedure recommended by the *Ancrene Riwle* (ed. M. Day, EETS 225, London, 1952) seems particularly relevant to the Pentangle Knight: 'Þer efter sech al ut 7 to trodde þine sunnen bi þine vif wittes. Þer efter bi alle þe limes þet tu hauest mide i suneged' (p. 154).

16 *John Gaytryge's Sermon*, ed. N. F. Blake in *Middle English Religious Prose* (York Medieval Texts), London, 1972, p. 81.

17 The point is made clearly at 3a. 90, 2: '. . . sin can take place in the heart alone by internal consent, as is clear from the *Secunda Pars*'. The reference is to 1a2æ. 72, 7.

18 Cf. *Jacob's Well*, p. 136.

19 Cf. Aquinas, *Summa*: 2a2æ. 66, 6.

20 Suspicion that Gawain may have fallen into Sloth may remind us of the dangers inherent in his lying *lurked* in the safety of the bedroom during the hunt with its healthy vigour and more explicit dangers. And it may add further significance to his association with the fox who, allegorically, dens in the human heart where, as Pride, he fathers the other Deadly Sins upon the vixen Sloth (see above, p. 66).

21 See, respectively, Chaucer, Parson's Tale, X, 1015; *Cursor Mundi*, ed. R. Morris, EETS 57, 59, 62, 66, 68, 99, 101, London, 1874–93, II, l. 11530; *The Siege of Jerusalem*, ed. E. Kölbing and M. Day, EETS 188, London, 1931, ll. 689–724; John Lydgate, *The Fall of Princes*, ed. H. Bergen, EETS ES 121–4, London, 1918–19, VIII, ll. 1464–1708; *Legends of the Saints in the Scottish Dialects of the Fourteenth Century*, ed. W. M. Metcalfe, STS, 13, 18, Edinburgh, 1896, XII, ll. 231–46; Chaucer, *Canterbury Tales*, VIII, ll. 1001–9. In a fifteenth-century translation of the *Legenda Aurea* (ed., in part, N. F. Blake, *Middle English Religious Prose* (York Medieval Texts), London, 1972) the Devil speaks of Julian as his instrument in tormenting the saints, and says of Judas: '. . . he did the treson that I counceylid hym . . .; By my Judas I have wonne many a soule' (p. 160). Julian and Judas are ranked with Cain amongst the Nine Unworthies, antitypes of the heroes of antiquity and romance (Dickins, pp. 228–32).

22 Robert Henryson, 'The Fox and the Wolf' in *The Poems and Fables of Robert Henryson* (ed. R. H. Wood, Edinburgh, 1933), l. 670. Henryson's fable, intended as a warning to those who, though they may express contrition, are unable to refrain from sin, tells how the Fox goes to Friar Wolf to confess his thefts but, since he feels no repentence, cannot promise amendment or do penance.

23 '. . . the fox signifies the hypocrite, to secular (as opposed to fraternal) writers a friar, and mystically the Devil' (R. P. Miller, 'Allegory in *The Canterbury Tales*' in *Companion to Chaucer Studies* (ed. Rowland, Oxford, 1968), p. 272). See above, pp. 65–6.

24 Honorius of Autun, *Speculum ecclesiae* (twelfth century), cited in Watkins, *History of Penance*, pp. 742–3. See also Nicholas Love, *The Mirrour of the Blessed Lyf of Jesu Christ*, ed. L. F. Powell, Oxford, 1908,

p. 207 and *The Southern Passion*, ed. B. D. Brown, EETS 169, London, 1927, pp. 859–66.

25   Some critics, finding such lightheartedness inconsistent with abuse of confession by a man of Gawain's devotion, argue: 'His joy is depicted as consequent on the absolution, which means that the absolution was valid (TGD, p. 123; *cf.* Foley, p. 73). But there are obvious dangers in judging moral awareness from external appearances, witness Gawain's use of the sign of the cross in his pantomime of surprise on the Lady's first entrance to his bedroom.

26   Is the poet, perhaps, suggesting the narrow line which separates tact from self-deception, such as, Donner suggests, Gawain practises in not mentioning the girdle at the exchange: '. . . as if by not actually denying the girdle he will be less guilty of deceit, as if there were a difference between a spoken and an unspoken lie. So long as he can avoid confronting the issue, he can continue to believe himself a virtuous man. The pretence by which he does so amounts to self-deception of the pettiest kind, so petty that it should be comic . . . (p. 314).

27   They have suggested to some that Gawain has abandoned hope of salvation through grace to seek safety by personal merit. 'When Gawain places his faith in God and depends upon His mercy and grace for safety and salvation, he is a knight of the shield. When he places faith in himself and attempts to secure his safety through his own efforts, he is a knight of the sash' (Champion, p. 421). Champion sees the interpretation of the theme as conforming to the generally conservative attitude to the fourteenth-century controversy between the orthodox Bradwardine and the neo-Pelagian Ockham displayed elsewhere in the work of the *Gawain*-poet.

28   R. J. Spendal, pointing out that Aquinas (*Summa*: 2a2æ. 58, 4) defines justice (sometimes called *veritas*, truth) in terms which can be equated with the chivalric virtues of the fifth pentad of the pentangle, suggests that, having failed to give Bertilak his just due, Gawain can no longer claim the symbol of *trawþe* as his spiritual emblem.

29   'Þe inre uondunge is twouold, fleshlich 7 gostlich; fleslich ase of lecherie, 7 of glutunie, 7 of slouhðe; gostlich as of prude, 7 of onde, 7 of wreððe. . . . also as of ȝiscunge' (*Ancrene Riwle*, p. 86).

30   'The god may be the beast that baits the man, or it may be the god that makes of the man his victim, either as possessed hunter or as captured object.' 'Before or after the general destruction, however, there may be a moment of recognition, an acknowledgement of the wrong done, or a stunning confrontation with the godhead' (Thiébaux, *Stag of Love*, pp. 58–9).

IV THE PURGATION OF TREASON

In studies on the work of the *Gawain*-poet it has generally
been assumed that 'alone of the four poems, *Sir Gawain and
the Green Knight* does not propound any explicit theological
message' (Turville-Petre, p. 33). Yet its social message of the
interrelations of chivalric idealism and human imperfection
has been recognised as implicit rather than explicit. I would
suggest that a related theological theme of divine mercy and
human blindness is implicit in the penitential element in the
poem. That element is established long before Gawain's confession at Hautdesert. The poem begins on New Year's Day,
the Feast of the Circumcision commemorating Christ's first
shedding of his blood for man, a prefiguration of baptism
(Levy, pp. 69–70), that sacrament in relation to which
penance is 'a second plank after shipwreck' (Aquinas,
Summa: 3a. 84, 6) in which sinful man seeks the redeeming
power of Christ's passion. The frequency with which some of
the pentads of the pentangle, especially the five wits, figure in
Middle English penitential manuals suggests a conscious
association of Gawain's idealism with confessional doctrine
(Ackerman, pp. 254–63); partly, perhaps, as an ironic reminder of man's fallibility and God's compassion. That the pentangle represents aspiration rather than achievement is recognised by Gawain himself who *cryed for his mysdede* (760) on
his winter journey, in a prayer of a traditional penitential
character (Burrow, p. 53). Burrow notes the association of
winter, with its warning of human mortality, and especially of
the winter journey, with such penitential scenes as the Good
Friday episode in Wolfram's *Parzival*. Gawain sets out to seek
the Green Chapel on All Souls' Day, having attended, with
ominous suitability, the Requiem Mass of that day, and jour-
neys through Advent when the Medieval Church celebrated

not only Christ's first coming but also his final coming at the Last Judgement (Burrow, pp. 54–5), until Christmas Eve finds him beyond that godless *wyldrenesse of Wyrale* reminiscent of the sin-haunted wilderness of man's earthly pilgrimage.[1]

When, after the Christmas interlude at Hautdesert, filled with seemingly innocent games, Gawain's journey is renewed on another New Year's Day, these associations are revived with an added significance. If, with Gawain's assumption of the role of the fox, we begin to suspect that he has become the victim of the sacred hunt, we may also be reminded that in medieval literature the metaphorical chase often became a journey in which the protagonist, sometimes hunter, sometimes quarry, was drawn 'ineluctably on his course from known surroundings into an unfamiliar, unsuspected, or forbidden territory where a crucial contest would take place, one that would change his life'.[2] To our earlier conception of Gawain the knight-errant (see above, pp. 19–20) as Everyman on his journey to death, subject like the brute creation to the forces of Nature, calling upon God for spiritual rather than bodily comfort, is now added the suspicion that, out of concern for his bodily safety, he has levelled himself morally with the beasts and is being divinely led or driven further into the wilderness to death and the Judgement beyond. The effect of this fusion of hunt and journey, even if only dimly sensed, is to contrast the hero's spiritual condition on his way to Hautdesert with that on his onward passage to the Green Chapel: has adoption of the green girdle in any way affected his faith in the values represented by the pentangle; is he conscious of any inconsistency between his penance and its possession; has it altered his relationship to God?

Superficially there is no apparent change: he still evokes the deity with every appearance of sincerity, swearing '*bi þe rode*', that symbol of redemption, as he hastily ends the incomplete Exchange of Winnings (1949); calling on the Lord to reward his hosts and their retinue (2052–7); commending the castle to Christ (2066–7), apparently unconscious of having been exposed to temptation there; crossing himself as he rides away (2071), reminding us, perhaps, of the same sign sincerely used at the first appearance of the castle and insincerely in deceiving the Lady. Like the latter gesture, all this is characteristically courteous and tactful. But is it entirely devoid of irony; or, by evoking earlier uses of the sign, is the poet reminding us of the narrow line which divides tact from deceit, formal observance from self-deception?

The contrast between the courtly, if deceptive, castle interior and the wintry wilderness is revived by a highly-wrought descriptive passage (2077–83), in which all the stressed syllables except one alliterate (Turville-Petre, pp. 56–7). But on this journey Gawain is no longer alone with God; the Guide given him by Bertilak accompanies him as a personification of the danger inherent in the Exchange of Blows and the temptation associated with the Exchange of Winnings. By his description of the denizen of the Green Chapel (2091–117) as malign and merciless, sparing neither knight nor churl, regular nor secular cleric, he revives the threat to courtly values which entered the romance with the challenge at Camelot and will now mount in intensity until Gawain, Camelot's representative and the exemplar of chivalry, faces the return blow at the chapel. The portrait is not a falsification of the earlier one, but a selective version ignoring the attributes of the knight-challenger and describing behaviour appropriate to the *wodwos*, darkened to suggest Death who slays all orders of men (Burrow, pp. 120–2). The unstated source of his knowledge has given rise to speculation on the Guide's identity, including the suggestion that he is Bertilak in yet another shape (Gollancz, p. xxxvi), or is in his confidence (Waldron, p. 11); but the ambiguity of his identity, like the combination of helpfulness and faintly contemptuous familiarity in his manner, probably reflects his ambivalent role in relation to the hero. Having failed to terrify him, he tempts him with an opportunity to avoid the return blow by flight (2118–28), promising '*I shal lelly yow layne*' in an ironic echo of the promise exacted from Gawain to conceal the girdle from Bertilak (Delaney, p. 251). Gawain's firm rejection shows no awareness that he is passing judgement on his own earlier behaviour (Mills, p. 629):

> . . . þat lelly me layne I leue wel þou woldez.
> Bot helde þou hit neuer so holde, and I here passed,
> Founded for ferde for to fle, in fourme þat þou tellez,
> I were a knyȝt kowarde, I myȝt not be excused.   (2128–31)

Has he genuinely changed his opinion that *My3t he haf slypped to be vnslayn, þe sle3t were noble* (1858), or is he merely
ashamed to be complicit with a servant in doing what he did
with the compliance of the Lady?

Outwardly his tone is determined – '*I wyl to þe chapel*' – and
his faith declared: '*Ful wel con Dry3tyn schape / His
seruauntez for to saue*'. But his reference to *chaunce þat may
falle* there, to the *talk* he will have with the Green Knight, and
his ambiguous use of *þe wyrde* ('fate' / 'the will of God' –
Waldron, p. 121) undermine the confident exterior. The contemptuous and fatalistic words of the Guide's dismissal
(2140–55) contain what may be ironic reminders of the issue
of values raised by the Exchange of Winnings ('*For alle þe
golde vpon grounde*') and the price, spiritual as well as
material, which Gawain may have to pay for the girdle ('*And
þe lyst lese þy lyf*'), raising echoes of Mark VIII, 36 (see above,
pp. 104–5). Set against this, Gawain's public manner is reminiscent of the stiff upper lip with which he faced his companions
on leaving Camelot (see above, pp. 16–17), but once alone,
when tact can only be a means of self-deception, he appears
equally resolute and dedicated:

> 'Bi Goddes self,' quoþ Gawayn,
> 'I wyl nauþer grete ne grone;
> To Goddez wylle I am ful bayn,
> And to hym I haf me tone.'   (2156–9)

How are we to judge this? As wholly sincere? – an indication
that Gawain puts no faith in the girdle (Howard, p. 238); or
that he regards its retention as a sin against the chivalric
rather than the Christian code, somehow disassociated in his
mind (Delaney, p. 253). As spiritual presumption? – since
'the hypocrisy of his confidence in God at this point undercuts
the virtue of his denial of the coward's flight' (Taylor, p. 10).
Or as sincere in intention, but morally obtuse? – Gawain
having recognised the straightforward choice between honourable courage and dishonourable cowardice, but not the
ethical conflict between his pentangle code and possession of
the girdle (Spearing, p. 226), between publicly acknowledged
principles and private motives (Waldron, p. 12); or, I would
add, between conscious conviction and instinctive reaction.

So, once again, Gawain comes in dubious moral state to a chapel (2160–96); and at first does not recognise it as such. Presented as an emanation of Nature, an outcrop from the rugged landscape, *nobot an olde caue*, it both surprises and disappoints (Burrow, pp. 122–3). For contemporary readers some of the sinister associations of such a location, a barrow by a waterfall, traditionally dragon-defended, might be operative here (Evans, p. 723), but there is no indication that the poet is using them thematically rather than atmospherically. Rather, they lend colour to Gawain's Christian judgement of the place: '*Here myȝt aboute mydnyȝt / Þe dele his matynnes telle!*'. In contrast to those earlier occasions when his opinion of the events in which he was caught up could only be guessed at (see above, pp. 13–15 and pp. 16–17), he now expresses openly, though in solitude, his judgement of the Green Knight and the Exchange of Blows compact:

> 'Wel bisemez þe wyȝe wruxled in grene
> Dele here his deuocioun on þe deuelez wyse.
> Now I fele hit is þe fende, in my fyue wyttez,
> Þat hatz stoken me þis steuen to strye me here.'
>
> (2191–4)

His response, at this stage, to the demonic associations of the Green Knight which readers may have sensed at his first appearance, his identification of the chapel as a place of evil and of himself as a chosen victim suggest an attitude of stoic despair rather than Christian confidence. The irony of his appeal to human judgement, one of the pentads of his slighted pentangle, and the memory of what may have been another *chapel of meschaunce* at Hautdesert if his *fyue wyttez* proved an inadequate safeguard against evil there imply possible, and possibly unconscious, causes of such despair. The reader alert to the patterning of the poem must see the Green Chapel in relation to the chapels at Camelot and Hautdesert and its obvious falseness as questioning the sincerity of the observances there (Hughes, p. 231). His own suspicions regarding the confession at Hautdesert may make him wonder whether Gawain's reaction here arises from the ominous atmosphere of the place, or from an uneasy conscience. And he may wonder also whether Gawain recognises that, just as the confessional is a place of judgement, this *corsedest kyrk* may be a place of retribution, demonic or divine.

The arrival of the testing agent (2197–234); is heralded, as at Camelot, by a strange, half-recognisable noise (2199–204; *cf.* 132–6): like the rasping of a grindstone, raising memories of the Green Knight's axe; yet described in terms which echo all the violent sounds of nature in the poem (Benson, p. 200), evoking the clamour raised by Bertilak's culling (*cf.* 1165–6; 1426–7; 1721–2). Ironic echoes of the Temptation invade the Beheading plot, reminding us of three types of instinctive response by which human nature might lead Gawain to level himself with the brute creation in breaking the terms of the Exchange of Blows: panic-stricken flight, violent resistance, and wily deceit. Gawain's continued submission to the divine will – '*Let God worche*' – rejects all three equally, and his conscious response is a shouted challenge, a *ȝelpyng* which brings his adversary whirling down upon him from the crag above. In appearance and nature the Green Knight is as ambiguous as before, vaulting sportively across the intervening stream on the haft of his axe, whose grim, four-foot blade dominates the scene from Gawain's point of view.[3] In the preliminaries to the return blow (2235–58), the courteous knight-challenger replaces the mocking axe-sharpener, welcoming Gawain as a man of his word and reminding him of the formal terms of their compact. But there is grim irony in his greeting – '*God þe mot loke!*' – and his acknowledgement of the hero as a '*truee mon*'; and an answering irony in Gawain's consciousness of body and soul as, swearing by God '*þat me gost lante*', he stipulates that only a single blow be struck. But is his stoic calm as he bares his neck, *And lette as he noȝt dutte*; / *For drede he wolde not dare*, real or feigned, inspired by faith in God or in the girdle?

Our doubts heighten the tension of the scene in which the blow is struck (2259–314); death seems certain, implying the death of the soul if retention of the girdle has involved conscious profanation of the sacrament of penance. Tension is prolonged by the two preliminary feints and Gawain's reaction to them. At the first he *þat doȝty watz euer* flinches slightly, proving, to some minds, that he puts no trust in his talisman: 'if all his avowals of resignation to God's will had been mere vacuous hypocrisies concealing his faith in it, he would not involuntarily betray his fear' (Howard, p. 238; *cf.* Stevens, p. 78). But in that case might not his flinching suggest a less than perfect faith in God, querying more sharply the price which he has paid for a talisman in which he sees no worth? I agree with those who see it as an instinctive human reaction, as impulsive as the stab of fear which first made him grasp at the girdle in Hautdesert (Shedd, p. 10); but remembering the brute reaction of the fox with which that impulse was associated, one is left wondering whether, then as now, faith and reason were overwhelmed by a gust of animal passion. However slight, it brings a denial of Gawain's identity in a mocking echo of the words in which Bertilak's wife denied his amorous identity: *'Þou art not Gawayn'* (2270; *cf.* 1293, 1481 – Taylor, p. 11), and an implication of that charge of cowardice to avoid which he has endured hardships and temptations (2273; *cf.* 456, 2131), and has, perhaps, paid a price at which we can still only guess. Gawain suffers the rebuke patiently, but with a despairing *'þaȝ my hede falle on þe stonez, / I con not hit restore'* which shows that from the first blow at Camelot he has recognised the unequal conflict in which he is trapped, against unfair odds which might justify the use of a protective talisman – if knightly honour and Christian faith allowed.

He bows his head to the axe again, still asserting faith in the values of the pentangle – *'haf here my trawþe'* (2287) – and stands unflinching under a second feint; but whether with the brute courage of the boar, as an image from insensate nature might suggest (2293–4), or with faith in God or the girdle, we cannot tell. Again the Green Knight's mockery reminds him that it is his chivalric reputation which is at stake,[4] but this time Gawain's courteous tact is swept away by an instinctive outburst of anger. A reaction of courage or despair in one *Þat hoped of no rescowe* (2308)? Despair of physical succour or spiritual salvation (*OED rescue* n., 1 'succour, deliverance'; *cf. rescue* v., 3 'to deliver from some evil or harm')? Grim-faced, the Green Knight raises his axe for the third time, but Gawain stands unflinching with the patience of a martyr for whom death is an affirmation of faith (McClure, p. 381). If the Green Knight's purpose has been to drive him to panic as he did the members of the Round Table (241–5, 315), or to reckless resistance as he did Arthur (319–22, 326–31) – and the beheading of deer and boar suggests what the outcome of such behaviour would have been (McClure, pp. 381–4) – he has failed. But if the third repetition of the hunting pattern works by inversion in the Beheading plot as in the Temptation one, what punishment will be visited by this agent of retribution upon a thief who may have secured his spoils by spiritual treason? The axe falls in bathetic anti-climax, doing no more than graze (*snyrt*) Gawain's neck, leaving a drop of blood on the snow at his feet.

The hero's immediate reaction (2315–30) is to fall into a defensive posture, shouting his defiance in a speech incoherent with jumbled emotions (Waldron, p. 129). Gawain is himself again, a knight with a knight's physical resources, freed from the ambiguity of games and wagers, like a man reborn:

> Neuer syn þat he watz burne borne of his moder
> Watz he neuer in þis worlde wyȝe half so blyþe   (2320–1)

We recognise the naturalness of such feelings in one who has escaped from death, but the image of the new-born child, with its reminder of the shriven soul as a soul reborn (Burrow, p. 132), queries their source: the justified confidence of the sanctified; the triumph of one who relies solely on his own prowess at the failure of an enemy to exploit his advantage; the instinctive relief of one who, like the fox, *Went haf wylt of þe wode with wylez*, at the success of his protective talisman? The ambiguity is given ironic force by the fact that Gawain's outburst is triggered by his own blood shining on the snow, potentially an emblem of punishment for sin and of the source of redemption for sinners (*cf.* Longo, p. 76). Superficially all seems well, but the extent to which we share the hero's relief and joy must depend on our awareness of such undertones and our previous judgement as to whether the greatest danger from the Green Knight's axe was to Gawain's body or his soul.

His opponent's reaction, though in direct contrast, is still more unexpected (2331–68): leaning on his axe in relaxation, admiring Gawain's knightly stance, *armed, ful aȝlez*, playfully mocking his over-reaction. The ambivalence of laughter throughout the poem, the frequency with which it has been undercut by the threat of aggression, the uneasy parallelism between the Green Knight's grim game and the social sports at Hautdesert with their undertones of violence, inhibit immediate response. Slowly, guided by tone, we recognise a fusion of Bertilak's human warmth with the authority exercised both by him and by the Green Knight. And, as the interdependence of the two Exchange compacts is revealed, we realise that, despite their professed admiration of chivalric values, both *personae* have somehow been complicit in a plot which threatened the death of a peerless knight and has achieved his humiliation. The cruelty of their sports, the unfairness of the test (*asay*, 2362) imposed by their games, should move our sympathy for Gawain; and yet there is something ludicrous in the position of one who has been 'had' which alienates us from him. Worse still, whatever our opinion of this composite personality, we are compelled to admit the justness of the judgement he now passes on Gawain – '*here yow lakked a lyttel, sir, and lewté yow wanted*' – so far as his retention of the girdle is concerned, since we too accept the maxim '*Trwe mon trwe restore*'. But how much does this ambiguous figure know of the circumstances of its retention? The judgement may be a legal one on the breach of the Exchange of Winnings compact, but the terms used evoke echoes of treason (*MED leaute* n., (*b*) 'loyalty, faithfulness'), *trawþe*, and restitution (*OED restore* v., 1 'to make return or restitution; 4(*a*) 'to free from the effects of sin'). Our minds are being directed to the wider moral issue involved in Gawain's fault.

His own response (2369–88) is an ironic reversal of the burst of action which followed his apparent escape from his doom: stunned silence, inner mortification, violent physical symptoms of shame, then an impulsive ejaculation:

> 'Corsed worth cowarddyse and couetyse boþe!
> In yow is vylany and vyse þat vertue disstryez.' (2374–5)

As his first, instinctive recognition of his fault it accords with the facts as we know them – that cowardice in the face of death made him covet another's property – but he cannot yet frame the accusation in personal form, and his assessment of the offence is expressed in general moral terms. Yet Burrow (pp. 127–30; *cf.* Foley, p. 78) sees here sufficient signs of contrition to satisfy the first condition for valid penance, and in the remainder of the episode other penitential formulae. First, restitution; but in what a spirit! Gawain angrily throws the belt to the Green Knight with '*Lo! þer þe falssyng, foule mot hit falle!*', unconsciously echoing Bertilak's comment ('*þe fende haf þe godez!*') on the worthlessness of its symbolic counterpart, the fox-skin, and confounding his own behaviour (*MED falsing* ger., (*a*) 'deceitful or treacherous dealing') with the innocent agent of his downfall ('also something that deceives or misleads'). Can he have forgotten the value he once put on it, or the price he paid to keep it? The forms are those of penance, but where is the *caritas*, the sorrow for sins which should inform them? The 'confession of mouth' which follows begins with personal admission of the faults already recognised, cowardice and covetousness, but in chivalric rather than moral terms, as failings in knightly integrity, offences against *larges* and *lewté*, the *fraunchyse* and *felaȝschyp* of the Pentangle. Then comes what seems 'a passionate and haphazard piling-up of moral terms' (Burrow, p. 129):

> 'Now am I fawty and falce, and ferde haf ben euer
> Of trecherye and vntrawþe: boþe bityde sorȝe
>   and care!
>   I biknowe yow, knyȝt, here stylle,
>   Al fawty is my fare;
>   Letez me ouertake your wylle
>   And efte I schal be ware.'   (2382–8)

There is still the same intemperate indirection, reviling the sin and not the sinner; the condemnation is sweeping but still imprecise; yet it ends with what are recognisably the formulae of confession, request for penance, and promise of amendment. And in response the confessor laughs!

There are puzzling elements in this 'confession' which continue to trouble commentators in spite of a general assumption that Gawain, realising for the first time that he had committed a fault in retaining another's property, makes the injured party his lay confessor in order to purge his sin immediately. If, still reeling from the shock of learning that the man whose blow he so feared that he took the green lace for protection represents himself as its rightful owner, knows of his theft, and reproaches him for his failure to *restore*, Gawain is able to think of his obligation to him, he might well consider that he owes him an explanation, an apology, the return of his property – but why a formal confession? To put concern for his own soul before his duty to others is contrary to his habitual courtesy and tact, if petty theft is all that he has on his conscience. But in that case the terms in which he states his fault must seem exaggerated and ambivalent: *fawty* (*MED fauti* adj., 2(*a*) 'failing in duty or moral rectitude; guilty of wrongdoing or sin'); *falce* (*MED fals* adj., 1(*a*) 'of persons, animals (specif. the fox, lapwing) etc.: deceitful, full of guile, guilty of breach of trust, faithless, disloyal, perfidious, treacherous'; 7(*b*) 'not adhering to approved Christian doctrines and practices'). He accuses himself, by implication, of *vntrawþe* – but is his offence against the social values of the pentangle or its Christian basis ? – and of *trecherye* – but treason to man or to God? Superficially, Gawain's perfectionist aspirations may explain why he sees any breach of *trawþe* as totally distorting the pentangle (Spearing, p. 209); yet his self-accusation seems extravagant to the point of comedy (Spearing, p. 227). But before we accuse him of scrupulosity (Tristram, p. 32), should we not consider that he may know more of the nature of his fault than we?

That he is in sin is manifest: theft and retention of the girdle must mean that his confession at Hautdesert was, consciously or unconsciously, incomplete. It is, I believe, Gawain's abrupt realisation of his abuse of the sacrament which accounts for the intensity of his mortification, the shocked incoherence and initial reluctance to face the moral implications, the extreme terms in which he eventually admits his fault and, above all, the penitential formulae he uses in doing so. It is as though sudden awareness of the danger in which his soul as well as his body had been under the Green Knight's axe has plunged him from passionate joy at the escape of the one to despairing anguish over the peril of the other; as though his first coherent impulse were to claim the cleansing power of the sacrament he has abused, an act as instinctive and unreflecting as his use of the sign of the cross on first facing the ambiguous Lady, his acceptance of the girdle, even, perhaps, his confession at Hautdesert. In each case his behaviour must be judged on the intention behind his act, but in the earlier instances we are given only a momentary glimpse of the inner man reflecting on circumstances and contemplating action (1195–9; *cf.* 1855–8), then acting in a consequential but – superficially judged – quite innocent way (1200–1; *cf.* 1859–65), then in a way which may profane a sacred sign or sacrament (1202–3; *cf.* 1874–82) – the evidence of intention is hypothetical not conclusive. Here, too, we are left to make our own judgement of the outer man: if his confession at Hautdesert was knowingly false, then Gawain's behaviour ever since – his Christian oaths and invocations of the deity, the blessings invoked on the castle and its inhabitants, his avowed trust in God when rejecting the Guide's escape offer, on his solitary journey, and in the face of his adversary at the Green Chapel (see above, pp. 114–18) – is a record of blasphemy and cynical hypocrisy. But then a man who has levelled himself with the fox as a thief may be expected to display the other moral attributes of the beast. And if we doubt his sincerity in what followed that confession, we may begin to question appearances in what preceded it – his piety, self-sacrifice, and trust in divine guidance – until the pentangle seems to represent a tissue of hypocrisy and deception. Yet the taking of the girdle – as, in a lesser sense, the sign of the cross – was in defence of the values of the pentangle and the reputation it represents, that the Pentangle Knight might not prove *a kny3t kowarde*. Now that reputation is under attack at the most fundamental moral level; and the accuser is the knight himself. If we doubted his sincerity in defence of his reputation, can we doubt it now when he exposes it to the judgement of the man he has offended, as to a new confessor?

Despite his laughter, the Green Knight's response suggests that he accepts his confessional role:

> 'Þou art confessed so clene, beknowen of þy mysses,
> And hatz þe penaunce apert of þe poynt of myn egge,
> I halde þe polysed of þat ply3t, and pured as clene
> As þou hadez neuer forfeted syþen þou watz fyrst borne'
>
> (2391–4)

– but in game or in earnest? He may merely be responding playfully to something Gawain intends seriously (Burrow, p. 132), the one expressing contrition and a disposition to confess, the other a layman's assessment of his spiritual state as a venial sinner who, having confessed, made restitution, and suffered bodily mortification by way of penance, may be considered absolved from sin.[5] But what does the 'confessor' understand his penitent's *ply3t* (*OED plight* n. 1, 1 'peril, danger'; 2 'sin, offence, guilt') to have been? Is his laughter benign indulgence for all human frailty, or mockery of the seriousness with which Gawain speaks of a sin whose true nature he cannot know?

The general function of this second, playful, confession is, I take it, to raise again the issue of the validity of the first, and lead the reader to consider Gawain's spiritual condition after this new 'absolution'. As with many of the other games in the poem, if one party is playing the other is in deadly earnest; the presentation, to my mind, is as deliberately ambiguous as that of Gawain's intention in taking the girdle and the validity of the confession which followed. Here, as there, the function of the ambiguity is not primarily to create narrative tension in preparation for a factual denouement, but to focus attention on moral issues which the reader must determine for himself. Like the other games, the confession at the Green Chapel has many external features of realism, but, as with them, it is the underlying intention which must constitute the reality, its sacramental validity. The essential factor is not the lay status of the confessor since, despite contemporary debate on the efficacy of confession to laymen, the Middle Ages acknowledged its value as containing the desire for priestly absolution.[6] 'God alone on his own authority absolves from sin' (Aquinas, *Summa*: 3a. 84, 3), and though the priest administers the form of the sacrament, 'internally prompted human acts supply matter, which is not supplied by the minister, but by God working interiorly' (3a. 84, 1). The first impulse of the penitent should, therefore, be to reject his sin before God, 'and he would grieve over his involvement, even if he were not to advert explicitly to it' (3a. 87, 1); this, together with 'some act with grace as its source, by which a man detests his sin either explicitly, or at least implicitly' –

such as striking the breast or reciting the Lord's prayer – serves for the removal of all venial sins (3a. 87, 3). But, since penance is a species of justice, it requires, in addition to grief for sin acknowledged, recompense from the offender and retribution from the one offended (3a. 85, 3), not, as in retributive justice, on the decision of a judge, but in accord with the will of the sinner seeking reconciliation in friendship with God against whom he has sinned (3a. 90, 2).

Against this background, Gawain's confession can be read as the instinctive impulse of a soul suddenly stricken with consciousness of guilt to acknowledge its sin openly and, at the same time, to make restitution to and accept retribution from the man materially injured by the offence. The Green Knight's response can be seen as having an equally ambivalent duality, with its half-amused acceptance of the twin roles of priest and judge and its interpretation of physical penalty as penitential retribution. The inner and outer forms of penance have been observed, though formal confession to a priest should follow later;[7] the renewed friendship between tester and tested has been celebrated in a final ritual game; all seems set for a conventional happy ending to the romance, confirming the validity of chivalric values.

But the fact that the Pentangle Knight has proved guilty of petty theft, the doubt consequently cast on the validity of his Hautdesert confession, and the extreme terms in which he now accuses himself undermine conventional expectations and compel further consideration of his spiritual state. If the petty theft were all, the impulse of grace to confess it before both those offended, God and man, should purge the venial sin involved. But if in turning to the temporal good represented by the girdle, Gawain has turned away from God, then he has committed a mortal sin deserving eternal punishment (Aquinas, *Summa*: 1a2æ. 72, 5). The repeated ironies, querying the value which Gawain sees in the girdle and the extent to which his reliance upon it undermines his trust in God, mock the impossibility that we, who know only the outer man, should judge the nature of his sin in taking it. We may deduce that he cannot have kept it without making a false confession, either consciously or unconsciously incomplete. The former, whatever its motive – shame, pride, despair – is deadly sin, offending against *caritas* and rejecting grace (see above, pp. 98–100). The latter possibility raises a host of queries which, without knowledge of Gawain's heart, we are powerless to answer (see above, pp. 97–8). 'There is no sin unless the act is ultimately controlled by the will' says Aquinas (1a2æ. 74, 2); but, all too often in human experience, emotion interferes with the operation of reason in estimating the justice of an act or the worth of an object: 'For the perception and estimation of reason is overwhelmed by a strong and unruly imagination and a distorted judgement of values' (1a2æ. 77, 2). When this happens, a man who knows in general terms what constitutes right and wrong may not recognise what is evil in a particular act or may be prevented by a 'gust of passion', some violent emotion, from properly weighing his actions: 'Thus a man can have habitual knowledge of both the general rule and the particular case, but fail to think about it at the moment' (1a2æ. 77, 2).

On this basis we might invent a scenario to explain how someone so high-principled and self-conscious as Gawain came to fall into sin: that, oppressed by fear of death, he was so overwhelmed by the prospect of escape offered by the girdle that he was momentarily incapable of appreciating the significance of accepting it, unable to weigh its value against that of the pentangle. But, without knowledge of the inner man, we cannot know to what extent he was ignorant of his own motives at the instant of acceptance, at the moment – then or later – when he decided to keep it, and on going to confession. Ignorance is a mitigating factor in sin only when it takes away knowledge which would keep one from sinning (1a2æ. 76, 1), but if it does not lessen free will it does not lessen sin (1a2æ. 76, 4). Gawain's ignorance, not of the nature of theft nor that the girdle does not belong to him but of his own intention respecting it, may mitigate his sin in so far as it was caused by some emotion which inhibited his self-will (1a2æ. 77, 6). But it cannot entirely excuse it since: '. . . no man is stirred by emotion and moved either to act sinfully or even deliberately consent to act sinfully with quite such swiftness. There is always time for deliberative reason to intervene and either suppress the emotion or inhibit its effect . . .' (1a2æ. 77, 8). Though we may suspect the swiftness with which the decision to take the girdle was made, even before the Lady's offer was complete (1861), the decision to keep it and to confess it or conceal it from the priest belong to the inner man and are beyond our determination. But remembering that preparation for confession involves the calm and ordered recollection of sinful acts and intentions (see above, pp. 93–4), we may feel that an imperfect confession argues moral blindness rather than emotional intemperance.

So though we may agree that Gawain has sinned, the degree and nature of his fault are not for us to judge. For the poet's purpose it is enough that his hero is now conscious of his sin. His own understanding of it, expressed in a calmer confessional version of his first outburst against *cowarddyse and couetyse* (2374):

'For care of þy knokke cowardyse me taȝt
To acorde me with couetyse, my kynde to forsake'
(2379–80)

has puzzled critics. *Cowardyse* may express not only lack of fortitude in the face of death, but also lack of that steadfastness which should inspire a Christian knight whose faith lies in God rather than magic talismans (Hunt, pp. 11–12). Desire for the girdle as worldly goods would be an offence against the poverty of a knight on a mission (Evans, pp. 730–1), but the poet has ironically stressed Gawain's refusal of it as one desiring *nauþer golde ne garysoun* (1837). Burrow (pp. 135–6) explains Gawain's self-accusation in terms of Aquinas' distinction (*Summa*: 1a2æ. 18, 6) between two aspects of a moral act: the external action (Gawain's theft of the girdle) and the end proposed by the will in doing it (in order to save his life), of which the former, objectively considered, is an act of covetousness; Lester (pp. 392–3) in terms of the trust he puts in a material object rather than God and his own powers. But within the basic moral sense of 'Avarice', the fifth deadly sin (*cf. MED coveitise* n., 1), are expressed many excesses of worldly desire and misuses of divine gifts, including that form of theft which, we have noted (see above, pp. 98–100), consists in abuse of the gift of grace, a form of apostasy seen in contemporary terms as spiritual treason, a breach of troth with God. Gawain's use of *couetyse* may,

therefore, be exact, acknowledging not only his materi
but his turning away from God to an object valued fo
rather than from love of God (Hunt, p. 12), and his reje......
conscious or unconscious – of sacramental grace in order to
retain it. If so, can he now accept a layman's 'absolution' for
the *trecherye and vntrawþe* (2383) into which he regards
himself as having fallen?

If one of the effects of penance, considered as an act of
justice, is to restore the state of *caritas* between the sinner and
God on one hand and the fellow-man he has offended on the
other, there seems to be something wrong in Gawain's post-
confessional state (2395–428). Urged to return to Hautdesert
and renew the New Year feasting, he refuses with a rueful '*I
haf soiorned sadly*' (*OED sadly* adv., 1(*b*) 'reluctantly'; 9
'grievously, deplorably'; *cf. sad* adj. and adv., 'having had
one's fill, sated, weary') and an ironic blessing: '*he ʒelde hit
yow ʒare þat ʒarkkes al menskes!*'. But to the suggestion of
reconciliation with the Lady '*Þat watz your enmy kene!*', he
responds with coldly formal greetings to both '*myn honoured
ladyez, / Þat þus hor knyʒt wyth hor kest han koyntly bigyled*',
and bursts into a bitter catalogue of famous men brought to
grief *þurʒ wyles of wymmen*. His antifeminism has been very
variously interpreted as a half-humorous defusing of his earlier emotional outburst, tactfully substituting the traditional
'eternal Eve' for the Lady as the cause of his downfall (Mills
(1970), pp. 635–40; Waldron, p. 134); a merely momentary
lapse in his courtesy (Brewer, pp. 77–8); a temporary effect of
the shock to his self-esteem of the discovery of his fallibility
(Burrow, p. 147; Evans, p. 732; Jacobs, p. 435); a desperate,
defensive gesture of hurt pride (Butturff, p. 146); an aban-
donment of his *cortaysye* (Engelhardt, p. 223) and, with it, the
whole system of courtly values expressed in his pentangle
(Spearing, pp. 223–4). The variety of interpretations suggests
that, as so often when the poet is working by indirection, it is
misleading to read one level of an ambivalent passage to the
exclusion of others. Gawain's thesis is that it is not to be
wondered at that a fool like himself should act stupidly
because of women when the greatest of the patriarchs were
beguiled by them. But the two commonplaces he evokes, both
foreign to romance tradition, are complex, and some of their

associations ironically undermine his argument. The exemplary types he cites were frequently used to illustrate both the possibilities and the limitations of human virtue, as warnings 'that no man truste in his owene perfeccioun, but he be stronger than Sampson, and hoolier than David, and wiser than Salomon' (Chaucer, Parson's Tale, X, 1955). The Solomon who figures here as the dupe of many women has already appeared in the poem as the originator of the pentangle (625); Gawain's self-association with the fallible exemplar of human wisdom ironically qualifies his own ideal status as the Pentangle Knight (Green, p. 53) – but is he aware of it? And his association of himself with those deceived by *wymmen þat þay vsed* evokes an irrelevant aspect of the antifeminist tradition; his *couetyse* was not for the Lady's person (*MED coveitise* n., 2 'strong sexual desire; lust'), but for her girdle, that ambiguous *drurye*, symbol of self-love. The smugness of his *'hit were a wynne huge / To luf hom wel, and leue hem not'* betrays the cause of his outburst; Gawain has not loved the Lady, but he has credited her account of the girdle and its powers, persuaded not by her wiles but by his own covetous desires. The echo of Adam's accusation against Eve and his inclusion amongst the deluded patriarchs typifies the confused logic of Gawain's argument, since for the medieval moralists Adam was the type of those who, by blaming others for misleading them, attempt to throw their sin upon God and their lack of free will.[8]

The indirection of Gawain's reasoning and the feebleness of his conclusion – *'Me þink me burde be excused'* – suggest to me his continuing reluctance or inability to admit, perhaps even to himself, the true nature of his guilt. One level of his mind advances, with superb tact, the conventional arguments of the old Adam; but how far is his tact self-deceptive, since the irrelevance of some terms and examples and the unintentional aptness of others undermines his rhetorical stance? Yet, as elsewhere, tact helps him to regain social balance after the intemperance of his first passionate outburst (Mills (1970), p. 640), and he is now sufficiently in control of himself to accept the girdle as a gift and ask his opponent's real name (2429–43). The explanation which follows (2444–66) of Bertilak's dual identity, his relationship to

Morgan le Fay, and her part in contriving the whole adventure appears to some critics unsatisfactory. Morgan seems to
them to enter the poem too late to embody effectively the evil
force behind the plot (Benson, p. 34); her hope that Guenevere would die of fright at the sight of the headless Green
Knight seems baseless; the source of her malign influence
over such a seemingly benign character as Bertilak remains
unexplained, as does the nature of his transformation into the
Green Knight. Neither imperfectly modified source elements
nor a casual attitude to plot motivation on the poet's part
(Benson, pp. 32–4) seems an adequate explanation; previous
experience has shown that when we accuse this poet of being
slipshod, the fault is often with our own perceptions. I would
suggest that here again the poet is playing upon romance
conventions for his own purposes. Morgan's hatred of the
Round Table and especially of Guenevere, and her misuse of
her magic powers against them, was a commonplace (Burrow,
pp. 125–6); the whole record of romance warns of her motive-
less malice and mysterious working. Our half-conscious feeling of resentment on Gawain's behalf at the lack of fair play in
his testing, the concealment of moral and physical threat
under courtly games, of a shape-shifter in courtly guise, the
moral key to a death struggle amongst bedroom badinage, is
irrelevant. The lesson of romance is that the very existence of
chivalry is a challenge to the forces of evil (Eadie, p. 300);
they lie in wait for knight-errants on every forest path, in
every wayside castle; their disguises are legion and their
methods devious. The poet has not cheated in marshalling the
conventions (McAlindon, p. 133); the Green Knight's moral
ambivalence is written on his person; Morgan enters the
poem hand in hand with her temptress and the rhetorical
contrast between them warns of the perils of the flesh (see
above, pp. 9–10); physical and moral danger threatens from
all sides – it is for the knight to penetrate its manifold disguises. The threat may come from within; Morgan's blood
runs in Gawain's veins (2464–7), as well as the blood of
Arthur on which he prides himself (357). And evil may come
from the perversion of good, as Morgan's black magic from
the powers which she obtained from Merlin by a deceptive
love (Barron, p. 178). 'Despite her unearthly powers, Gawain

is seen, and sees himself, to be the sole shaper of his destiny'
(Bercovitch, p. 35).

So, though he is calmer now, he rejects the invitation '*com
to þyn aûnt*' with an emphatic negative which suggests continuing bitterness, though whether against his tempters or
himself we cannot tell. His parting from Bertilak (2367–78),
as they exchange the kiss of peace and commend each other to
þe prynce of paradise, suggests that they at least are in charity
with each other. The poet's manipulation of Morgan's traditional role frees Bertilak from personal malignity and
demonic associations, leaving the validity of his judicial and
confessional role untouched. In retrospect we may see that
our concern as to his complicity with his wife, and how much
he knew of events in the castle during his hunting, is as
irrelevant as the mechanics of his transformation into the
Green Knight. He and his wife serve as occasions of evil, but
the evil is in Gawain's heart. Equally, it seems to me beside
the point to ask what Bertilak knows of Gawain's confession
at Hautdesert or his present penitential state. Our suspicions,
and the ambiguities of situation, characterisation, metaphor,
and language which stimulated them, now seem to have been
directed to moral and thematic rather than narrative ends.
His '*Trwe mon trwe restore*' may seem to introduce the penitential issue before Gawain's 'confession' to him at the Green
Chapel (see above, p. 121); or is it rather our concern for the
hero's spiritual state which colours his language? The power
of the testing agent, however mysterious, cannot penetrate
the heart of his victim or the secret of the confessional. We
must make our own judgement of Gawain's moral condition
and his awareness of the state of his soul.

As the Green Knight returns to his limbo, *Whiderwarde-
so-euer he wolde*, we are left to follow Gawain on his solitary
winter journey with its *mony aventure in vale* which threaten
body and soul (2479–83). The penitential implications of the
outward journey (see above, pp. 113–14) are not reinvoked,
though now again Gawain has *no gome bot God bi gate wyth
to karp* (696). If he has any sin upon his soul, the moment
seems right for one of those hermit confessors who inhabit the
waste-lands of romance (Smithers, pp. 171–2); the more so
since we know the ceremonial reception, the triumphant

announcement of success or humiliating confession of defeat, which awaits returning knight-errants at Camelot. Instead, we are told that, the wound in his neck having healed, *þus he commes to þe court, knyȝt al in sounde* (2489) – physically or spiritually?

The court before which he appears is the old, self-assured Camelot of the opening of Fitt I, evoked by the same conventional vocabulary (*wele, grete, gode, gayn, syker*); and its old-established custom is about to be fulfilled by *an vncouþe tale* as *ferlyly he telles, / Biknowez alle þe costes of care þat he hade*. Yet this is no mere tale *Of alderes, of armes*, but a confession echoing the terms of the confessions at Hautdesert and the Green Chapel (*biknowez, schewed*), and adding others with overtones of moral condemnation: *care* (*MED* n. 1, 3(c) 'sin, wickedness'); *blame* (*MED* n., 2(b) 'an offense, a sin'). The usages of chivalric romance are ironically fused with that form of public penance still practised in fourteenth-century England, and in which ecclesiastical discipline often reinforced secular justice by excommunicating those guilty of such moral breaches as perjury and treason.[9] But this penance is self-imposed, a seigniorial court such as the Round Table has no greater power to absolve than any layman, and Gawain's ambiguous use of confessional terms must raise again the question of his spiritual state.

Though his inner mortification is now partly suppressed by his social tact, his Camelot 'confession' is no more factually explicit and the terms of self-condemnation are still those used at the Green Chapel. Here, however, they are associated with the green girdle which assumes a new symbolic function. Violently rejected in the first shock of his self-knowledge as a *falssyng*, the agent of his deception, it was later gratefully accepted as a symbol of his own deceit:

> '. . . in syngne of my surfet I schal se hit ofte,
> When I ride in renoun, remorde to myseluen
> Þe faut and þe fayntyse of þe flesche crabbed,
> How tender hit is to entyse teches of fylþe;
> And þus, quen pryde schal me pryk for prowes of armes,
> Þe loke to þis luf-lace schal leþe my hert.'
>
> (2433–8)

– and the poet ironically reminds us of the ambiguous value it has previously borne, as the object of Gawain's *couetyse*, stolen for the preservation of his *prys*, by making him stress that it has no material worth for him *'For wele ne worchyp'*. Superficially, Gawain is here confirming the Green Knight's recognition of his real reason for valuing the girdle: *'for no wylyde werke, ne wowyng nauþer; / Bot for ȝe lufed your lyf'* (2367–8; *cf.* 2037–42); but also, perhaps, reacting in shame to his punning use of *wylyde*, referring both to the skilful workmanship of the embroidered garment and the cunning means and deceptive purpose by and for which he had purloined it. Superficially, too, he accepts it in the terms in which Bertilak offers it, as *'a pure token / Of þe chaunce of þe grene chapel at cheualrous knyȝtez'*; but, as with the green axe now hanging in the hall at Camelot, *bi trwe tytel þerof to telle þe wonder* (480), the meaning of the trophy may depend on who recounts the *chaunce* (*MED* n., 2 'a stroke of (good or bad) luck') associated with it. For Gawain the green lace is to be a memento of failure, a shameful rebuke to chivalric pride, a symbol of his transgression through excessive indulgence (*cf. OED surfeit* n., 2(*a*) and 3) of the weakness of the flesh whose retrograde nature (*cf. MED crabbed* ppl. (*a*) 'crablike'; (*b*) 'perverse, vicious, wicked') makes it so susceptible to infection by the plague spots of sin (*cf. OED tache* n. 1, 2 'a moral spot or blemish'). His language, echoing the analogy between sin and disease which was a commonplace of the medieval moralists (Waldron, p. 134), shows that for him the fault represented by the girdle was no mere breach of chivalric *lewté* to a fellow knight. For now, at last, he sees it as a *luf-lace*!

Since even the injured husband has rejected the amorous implications of the girdle, we are compelled to recognise that what Gawain is acknowledging is that love of self which lies at the root of all sin: 'Every sin arises from an inordinate desire for something good or from an inordinate escape from evil. However, both of these presuppose love of the self. For a man desires a good thing or shuns an evil because he loves himself' (Aquinas, *Summa*: 1a2æ. 77, 4). A properly directed love of self is both obligatory and right; it is this natural, God-given instinct to save his life which his temporal judge approves in Gawain (*'þe lasse I yow blame'*). But only Gawain can know in his heart how far love of life has caused him to turn away

from love of God. His self-accusation acknowledges that fear
of death on one hand dishonour on the other threw him into
that disorder of the emotions known to the moralists as pride
of life: 'The inordinate desire for goods which involves overcoming an obstacle belongs to the pride of life, in the sense
that pride is an inordinate attraction for some kind of
superiority . . . The pride of life includes cupidity in the sense
that cupidity ranges over the whole field of the desirable'
(Aquinas, *Summa*: 1a2æ. 77, 5). The manner in which he
wears the girdle as he rides away from the Green Chapel
shows his awareness of the part which chivalric pride played
in his downfall:

> Þe hurt watz hole þat he hade hent in his nek,
> And þe blykkande belt he bere þeraboute
> Abelef as a bauderyk bounden bi his syde,
> Loken vnder his lyfte arme, þe lace, with a knot,
> In tokenyng he watz tane in tech of a faute.
>
> (2484–8)

The obvious intention is to associate the belt with the wound,
to give permanent and visible form to the *penance apert*
received from his 'confessor', acknowledging his secret sin
before all the world (*cf. MED apert*, adj., 4(*a*) 'open, public').
In a moral system which saw bodily penance as a medicine
against sin and enjoined penitents to share the pains which
Christ endured for their redemption (*Ancrene Riwle*, p. 165),
the wound itself might be seen as the suffering of the head
being shared by a limb (p. 163). In association with it, the
girdle may suggest one of the 'arms of shrift' sanctioned by the
contemporary church – most commonly a hair-shirt (Burrow,
p. 151), but Gawain's method of wearing it gives it an ambivalent dual significance. Worn diagonally across his chest,
from right shoulder to left flank, it crosses the pentangle on
his surcoat like the heraldic 'bend' which differences a coat of
arms; indicating, to my mind, that Gawain no longer considers himself entitled to bear the symbol of *trawþe*.[10] At the
same time, by displaying openly the object of his *couetyse* he
does public penance both for his theft and his abuse of shrift,
as if in fulfilment of the *Ancrene Riwle*'s paraphrase of the
prophet Nahum: 'Þu noldest nout un-wreon þe to ðe preoste
ine schrifte, 7 ich chulle scheawen al nakedliche to alle uolcke

þine cweadschipes 7 to alle kinedomes þine scheomefule sunnen. ... 7 trussen al þi schendful-nesse oþine owune necke, ase me deð oþe þeoue þet me let forte demen' (*Ancrene Riwle*, p. 145). The trophy offered to Gawain as a chivalric memento now serves to associate him with the petty thief overtaken by public hue and cry (see above, pp. 73–4).

When, at Camelot, he is again *Among prynces of prys*, he displays it in the same ambivalent way:

> 'Þis is þe bende of þis blame I bere in my nek,
> Þis is þe laþe and þe losse þat I laȝt haue
> Of couardise and couetyse þat I haf caȝt þare;
> Þis is þe token of vntrawþe þat I am tan inne'

> (2506–9)

The mingling of heraldic and moral terms acknowledges both failure in a chivalric mission and moral flaw: *bende* (*MED* n. 1, 4); *token* (*OED* n., 8(*b*) 'armorial bearings, heraldic arms' (1562); 2(*b*) 'a spot on the body indicating disease' (1634)); *laþe* (*MED loth* n., 1(*a*) 'injury'; (*c*) 'fault'); *losse* (*MED los* n. 1, 2(*a*) 'defeat'; 1(*e*) 'forfeiture of God's love'; 3(*c*) 'banishment of Man (from Paradise)'). The admission of moral failure is as extreme – and oblique – as before. And the response is bathetic: *Þe kyng comfortez þe knyȝt, and alle þe court als / Laȝen loude þerat*, and all agree to wear the green lace like the ribbon of a chivalric order:

> For þat watz acorded þe renoun of þe Rounde Table,
> And he honoured þat hit hade euermore after,

> (2519–20)

Whatever they may have understood from Gawain's 'confession' of the nature of his fault, their association of the good name of the Round Table with what he sees as a token of *vntrawþe*, seems trivial and inadequate, like the courtiers' suggestion when he is facing death in the Beheading test that he be made a duke. Their language recalls the superficiality and moral inadequacy of Camelot in face of the Green Knight's challenge (see above, pp. 5–6); the memory of their behaviour at Gawain's departure, social tact covering moral indecision and duplicity (see above, p. 18), devalues their judgement on his mission, and queries their sincerity in associating themselves with its outcome (Butturff, p. 147;

Green, p. 61; Jacobs, p. 434; Taylor, p. 7). And on this occasion, Arthur's voice is joined with theirs. But the ironic undermining of the conventional close of Arthurian romance, with the values of the Round Table re-affirmed in ceremonial conclave, is neither explicit nor destructive; its function is to challenge our opinion of the various judgements passed on Gawain, by his peers, his opponent, and by the hero himself.

The court's unreflecting eagerness to associate themselves with him in glory or dishonour contrasts with Berilak's estimate of him as peerless:

> 'On þe fautlest freke þat euer on fote ȝede;
> As perle bi þe quite pese is of prys more,
> So is Gawayn, in god fayth, bi oþer gay knyȝtez.'
>
> (2363–5)

High praise, but on a comparative and chivalric basis, evaluating Gawain as one knight among many. Yet the imagery used evokes memories of the pentangle with its *vertuus stonez*, blazon of a knight who aspired to perfect chivalry: the pearl, so often a symbol of perfection, superficially considered so similar to a dried pea yet so different in value; their contrasted *prys* suggesting the comparative worth of pentangle and girdle to a knight who chose to weigh honour against life, bodily safety against spiritual salvation. Bertilak recognises human failure as natural and excusable, and having forgiven Gawain for his lack of *lewté* can still honour him *'for þy grete trauþe'* (2470); but Gawain cannot forgive himself for the *vntrawþe* represented for him by the girdle. For those who accept Bertilak's judgement as rational and balanced, a necessary corrective of his victim's lack of *mesure* in self-knowledge as in chivalric aspiration (McClure, p. 386; Shedd, p. 10; Smithers, pp. 174–5), Gawain's self-condemnation must seem exaggerated to the point of comedy, a ludicrous failure to reconcile aspiration with achievement (Christmas, p. 242; Spearing, pp. 228–9). To Burrow the discrepancy is rooted not in the facts of the case but in the interpretative bias: 'For Bertilak the adventure demonstrates man's possibilities for good; for Gawain it demonstrates his possibilities for evil' (pp. 136–7). But this assumes that their disparate judgements are based upon the same facts, yet many years of critical controversy have not produced agreement on those facts, on the precise nature of Gawain's fault. I am not alone in feeling 'that a completely satisfactory account of the final scene between Bertilak and Gawain and, indeed, of the whole romance, has not yet been proposed' (Hunt, p. 13).

Any account which does not give weight to the hero's assessment of his spiritual condition must be suspect. From the moment when he agreed to take and conceal the girdle, or after his Hautdesert confession, or at the death of the fox, or on his failure to include the lace in the Exchange of Winnings, or when he casually juxtaposed it with the pentangle in arming himself for the Green Chapel – according to our moral perception – we have had reason to fear for his soul. From our observation of the outer man, we have been led to suspect that, threatened with loss of chivalric reputation on one hand and loss of life on the other, motivated by pride and self-love, he has consciously stooped to social deception in an act of theft and hardened his heart to spiritual treason in a false confession; or, alternatively, that his social duplicity was unconscious, an instinctive act inspired by a gust of passion, shame or fear, accompanied by moral blindness preventing consideration of his ultimate intention with respect to the girdle (breach of *cortaysye* towards the Lady by revealing her gift or of *fela3schyp* with Bertilak by retaining his property), and realisation of the need to confess any sinful intent. In either case the cause of sin may have been an act of free will or one influenced by the Devil operating upon the passions to present an object as desirable (Aquinas, *Summa*: 1a2æ. 80, 1–2) – as medieval readers, conscious of the Devil as a hunter of men's souls and familiar with the tradition of the mortal chase, might have been reminded by Bertilak's hunting. Equally, blindness and hardness of heart may be caused by the soul turning away from divine enlightenment or by God withholding the light of grace from those in whom he finds an obstacle to it, as a punishment or as a means of salvation, 'so that they might discover something from becoming sinners, and in this way become humbled and transformed' (1a2æ. 79, 4; *cf. Jacob's Well*, pp. 69–70) – possibilities which contemporary readers might associate with the tradition of the sacred

chase and the instructive cl
degree of Gawain's sin is, I hav
our investigation, since it dep
which we have no knowledge

Since we would naturally p
whom we have been led to ide
blindness rather than spiritua
signs of moral awakening, of al
Green Knight's revelation. We
between his instinct to confess a
perance of expression, the a
throwing blame upon the casu
natural, instinctive reactions in one faced with the failure of
his perfectionist aspirations. That this uncharitable spirit
should continue after he has received 'absolution' from the
man he offended, in his refusal to be reconciled to the ladies at
Hautdesert, is disturbing; so is his failure to seek formal
absolution from priest or hermit on his perilous journey to
Camelot. Yet, once there, he masters his shame to renew his
spiritual purgation, repeating his self-condemnation in the
same unvarying terms, and adopting an emblem of his failure
as a permanent penance. The predominant signs are those
which, I would suggest, medieval readers might interpret as
attrition, that spiritual condition described by the Council of
Trent as 'conceived commonly either from consideration of
the foulness of sin or from fear of hell and punishment' and
distinguished from that perfect contrition which is a pre-
requisite of penance 'in that its motives are less perfect than
the motive of charity, and that its efficacy is less perfect, for it
does not of itself reconcile to God'.[11] Both before Trent and,
indeed, to the present day, controversy sought to distinguish
between two motives for attrition: 'basely servile fear' incited
only by dread of punishment and selfishly unconcerned by the
evil of offending God; and 'simply servile fear' which, by not
explicitly excluding love of God, mitigates the sinful act as an
offence against a loving God. The latter, leading to detestation of sin as the greatest of evils to be avoided always and at
all costs, expresses *caritas* sufficient to reconcile the sinner to
God even before the sacrament is received, though not without including the desire for the sacrament.[12]

...usness of his sin burst upon Gawain at the ..., we have waited anxiously for him to seek ...solution. We have seen him moved by shame and ...penitential impulse expressed in two 'confessions' to ...e offended and to his own knightly fraternity, ask for ...d accept penance, and adopt in humility a badge of perpetual penitence:

> 'And I mot nedez hit were wyle I may last;
> For mon may hyden his harme, bot vnhap ne may hit,
> For þer hit onez is tachched twynne wil hit neuer.'
>
> (2510–12)

The penultimate line may be read at two levels, turning upon the double sense of *harm* already used by the poet (*MED* n., 1(*a*) and (*c*)): though man may conceal his guilt (as the girdle concealed Gawain's wound) he cannot undo the sinful act – acknowledging both the concealment of the object of his sin from Bertilak and his false confession at Hautdesert? But the final line, with its implication that his *vntrawþe* is irremediable (Margeson, pp. 18–19), as rooted in him as the elements of his *trawþe – which were fetled on þis knyȝt, / And vhcone halched in oþer, þat non ende hade* (656–7) – smacks of that despair which more angered God in Cain and Judas than their treason against him:

> Þyr ys no synne þat men of rede,
> So moche withseyþ þe godhede;
> For wanhope wenyþ þat þe foly
> Be more þan Goddes mercy.
>
> (Mannyng, *Handlyng Synne*, 12, 295–8)

The contemporary reader, however, might be conscious of a suppressed thought behind both lines: the first paraphrasing the opening of Proverbs XXVIII, 13, 'He that covereth his sins shall not prosper' (Burrow, p. 155), without admitting its conclusion 'but whoso confesseth and forsaketh them shall have mercy'; the second expressing the foulness of sin indirectly through terms which acknowledge the eternal punishment it deserves:[13]

> . . . the sinner sees his act as evil because it is the cause of the eternal penalty of hell, or of other punishments that follow on sin. . . . If this proceeds as it can to an effective detestation which excludes the will to sin and makes a

man turn to God with hope of pardon, then a man has that attrition defended by Trent . . .

(*Catholic Dictionary*, *s.v.* Attrition, p. 207)

The degree of Gawain's attrition is hidden in his heart; but he has not yet sought the sacrament of penance, without the desire for which even perfect contrition is insufficient for justification (*Catholic Dictionary*, *s.v.* Contrition, pp. 124–5). And he is not to speak again; 'In strictly theological terms, Gawain is still in a state of sin at the end of the poem – for he has made no sacramental atonement' (Burrow, p. 156).

A final ambiguity? But like the many which have preceded it, implying thematic possibilities to which guidance is provided not by the plot of the poem but by its rhetoric. For at the moment when Arthur's court relegates its emissary's bitter experience to the perspective of romance, the linear record of western chivalry runs back through *þe Brutus bokez* to the moment when, *After þe segge and þe asaute watz sesed at Troye* (2525), the archetypal hero *þat þe trammes of tresoun þer wroȝt* (3), tested under a double obligation, redeems his betrayal of one by an admirable deception, *þe trewest on erthe*, in the other, and survives to father the race which founded that New Troy where *boþe blysse and blunder* have succeeded one another ever since (David, pp. 404–7). By echoing its opening line at line 2525, multiple reminder of the five pentads of the symbol of *trawþe*, the poem connects the founding father with the Pentangle Knight who, through a petty deception for the preservation of his chivalric virtues, fell into a spiritual treason as yet unpurged. But the poem does not end there; its 101 stanzas, completing one cycle and beginning another (Turville-Petre, p. 68), suggest that the history of man has its steady cycles like the seasons (Tristram, p. 112), that *blunder* may turn to *blysse*, that, as readily as he turned from *trawþe* to *vntrawþe*, the traitor may become the truest on earth (David, p. 407). And the lines which extend beyond the historical circularity of the poem, offer, under the guise of the tritest of terminal conventions in minstrel romance, an escape from the inevitability of human error, a redeeming power forged by trial and suffering from mankind's most monstrous sin:

Now þat bere þe croun of þorne,
He bryng vus to his blysse! AMEN   (2529–30)[14]

A redemption which, in my submission, Gawain has still to
claim. If so, the poem ends as it has proceeded, not with
resolution but implication, not with a pat solution confirming
chivalric values, in the manner of conventional romance, but
in an enigma challenging reconsideration of their validity in
relation to human instinct on one hand and God's will for his
creation on the other (Taylor (1969), pp. 165–6), as in the
other works attributed to the *Gawain*-poet (Brewer (1967),
pp. 131–2). The reflection or re-reading to which the form of
the poem invites will not solve the enigma by detecting some
trick of plot which exculpates the hero by establishing the
unfairness of the test, or the malign intent of the testing-
agent, or the innocence of Gawain's intention in accepting the
girdle; nor, I think, would more intimate knowledge of
contemporary theology establish whether his Hautdesert
confession was consciously or unconsciously incomplete, or
whether the degree of his ultimate contrition is already sufficient for grace within the action or must await some fuller
degree of self-knowledge beyond it. The moral arena of the
poem is located in the hero's heart (Brewer (1967), p. 140),
to which our access is limited; but our knowledge of his acts is
sufficiently intimate to make us participants, challenged to
judge their outcome in the light of our own moral perception.

As readers of romance we accept that literature should
express human idealism in its most exalted form; in the aspiration of the Pentangle Knight we recognise an admirable
intermingling of Christian and chivalric values expressed in
absolute form. And when, under social test, those values are
brought into conflict with each other, we admire the tact and
skill with which *cortaysye* is balanced against *felaȝschyp*,
fraunchyse against *clannes*, without offence to the knight's
hosts or his own integrity. But when the issue becomes one of
life and death, we find it natural if not excusable, recognising
our own humanity in him, that absolute values should give
way to pragmatic ones, concern for reputation to love of life,
the sense of honour to the instinct for self-preservation
(Davenport, pp. 151–2). Gawain's need is so great, the girdle

so trifling, the moment of theft so indefinable, the moral implications so unclear, the proof of dishonest intent so long postponed, that we have no occasion to reflect that failure, however trifling, in any virtue of the pentangle is a distortion of the whole (Spearing, p. 198), that any breach of *trawþe* is *vntrawþe*, that thoughtless betrayal of trust between man and man may lead to spiritual treason, and that though the one may be venial the other is mortal sin.

Our own failure to identify the precise nature of Gawain's fault, the moment of its occurrence, its complex moral implications, all the elements which have puzzled critics, involves us in his humiliation. We experience vicariously the complex demands of *trawþe*, realise 'how the maintenance of *integritas* demands constant awareness of all competing claims on one, rather than a sort of linear concentration on a single test or temptation, for moral danger is many-sided' (Hunt, p. 2). But, with the advantage of literary perspective focussed by the poem's rhetoric, we detect dangerous signs of preoccupation with one aspect of reputation to the neglect of others, of fear of cowardice suppressing consciousness of theft, of natural impulse overcoming self-control. We may feel that the fault lies with the impossible demands made by Christian chivalry, involving fallible man in a perpetual struggle between *cupiditas* and *caritas*, pride and humility, temptation and virtue. But if the alternative is a too-ready, cynical acceptance of human weakness, we must respect an idealism in which failure is a matter for bitter regret.

It is this element in *Sir Gawain* which has so far been undervalued. Ignoring the extent to which the idealism of many other romances is undercut by irony, we have been so embarrassed by Gawain's failure that we felt the need to minimise it. Yet failure is surely an integral and positive component of the theme. The hero's reaction to it displays the same intemperance, the same impulsive yielding to passion – shame and anger – and, initially, the same reluctance to recognise personal responsibility as in the commitment of the original fault. The superimposition of the symbol of *vntrawþe* upon the pentangle, shows the same absolutism in self-degradation as in his former idealism. And from his failure to seek priestly absolution within the poem, we are led to fear that he is still in the grip of that spiritual blindness which caused him to turn from God to the girdle, or of that despair of divine mercy which is only another expression of the same sin of pride. For the Pentangle Knight to become for ever the Knight of the Girdle argues no advance in self-knowledge, no acceptance of human limitations, no understanding of the relation of fallible man to an all-forgiving deity.

But to read *Sir Gawain* as a tragedy of chivalric corruption and spiritual blindness would be to ignore its inherent message of the need for *mesure* in the face of man's capacity for good and evil. Gawain's intemperance under failure is gradually mastered by penitence, his reputation voluntarily exposed to public censure, his fault self-defined in both chivalric and spiritual terms; signs of contrition which give hope for the future. The pentangle has not been abandoned, merely occluded. And under both symbols, as sinner and as aspirant to *trawþe*, we have been invited to laugh at Gawain; in irony not ridicule, laughter which is neither sacrilegious in a medieval context, nor on our part destructive of idealism, since it rebounds upon ourselves. As though the poet were reminding us that, faced with our own humanity, our infinite capacity for good and evil, high aspiration and low cunning, self-knowledge and self-deception, we must laugh if only not to weep.[15]

NOTES

1   '. . . 7 ʒe mine leoue sustren wendeð bi þen ilke weie toward te heie ierusalem, to þe kinedom þet he haueð bihoten his icorene. Goð, þauh, ful warliche, vor iþisse wildernesse beoð monie vuele bestes: liun of prude, neddre of attri onde, vnicorne of wreoðe, beore of dead slouhðe, vox of ʒiscunge' (*Ancrene Riwle*, p. 87).

2   Thiébaux, *Stag of Love*, p. 56.

3   If Waldron (p. 125) is right that what seems a comparative assessment of the size of the blade (*Hit watz no lasse bi þat lace þat lemed ful bryʒt*) 'is an oath on the green girdle . . ., spoken *in petto* by Gawain', it is a significant acknowledgement that he sees it as a protective talisman. But the reference may be deliberately ambiguous, overtly applicable to the lace looped about the handle of the axe (*cf.* 217–20), but covertly reminding us of that other lace of green and gold.

4   His choice of terms – '*Halde þe now þe hyʒe hode þat Arþur þe raʒt*'

(2297) – may remind us of the wagers at Hautdesert as well as Camelot, and that he is as much the representative of the Round Table in one game as in the other (see above, p. 33, n. 7).

5   Noting the use of *polysed* to mean 'cleansed (of sin)' in *Cleanness* (1129–32; *cf*. 1068, 1134), Burrow (pp. 131–2) comments: 'The poet does not allow Bercilak to use the proper clerical term "assoil"; but it is clear that the term which he does allow him is one itself associated with the sacrament of penance – in the poet's mind, at least.'

6   See *Catholic Dictionary*, *s.v*.. Absolution, p. 15. Peter Lombard, in his *Sententiae* (1145–50) stipulates: '. . . confession should be made first to God and then to the priest', but adds '. . . yet, before the confession is in his mouth, if the intention be in his heart, forgiveness is accorded him' (cited in Watkins, *History of Penance*, p. 745).

7   'Lihte gultes beteð þus anonriht bi ou suluen, and þauh siggeð ham ine schrifte hwon ȝe þencheð of ham, ase ȝe spekeð mid preoste' (*Ancrene Riwle*, p. 156).

8   See Mannyng, *Handlyng Synne*, ll. 12339–410.

9   See T. P. Oakley, *English Penitential Discipline and Anglo-Saxon Law in their Joint Influence*, New York, 1923, pp. 76–86; *cf*. Burrow, p. 131, n. 25. There was often a similar mingling of confessional and judicial overtones in the appearance of returning knight-errants before a court of their peers: 'In the recounting of the knight's adventures before King Arthur's court we recognise the literary equivalent of an inquisitory deposition' (Bloch, *Medieval Law*, pp. 254–5). If detectable here, they may reinforce the parallel with Gawain's confession before the Green Knight and the judgement implicit in his response.

10   I am not suggesting a formal heraldic distinction, since the normal use of a bend as a difference was to distinguish the arms of members of the same family; here, as elsewhere, the poet is extending creatively elements of feudal usage familiar to his original audience. See A. H. St John Hope, *A Grammar of English Heraldry*, Cambridge, 1953, pp. 20–3 and pp. 60–1.

11   *Catholic Dictionary*, *s.v*. Attrition, pp. 206–7.

12   See *Catholic Dictionary*, *s.v*. Attrition, pp. 207–9, and *s.v*. Contrition, pp. 124–5.

13   *Tachched* suggests a word-play on *OED tache* v. 2, 2 'to lay hold of (a pers.)' and *tache* v. 1, (*a*) 'to stain or taint, esp. with moral defilement'.

14   The antithetical association of *blysse* and *blunder* in the historical frame surrounding Gawain's adventure may be intended to associate it with the *felix culpa*, the fall of Adam through which, paradoxically, salvation was provided for the sins of all mankind (see Haines). If so, the *vus* of the last line of the poem extends to all readers in every age the implication that if *blunder* is omnipresent in this world so is the redeeming power which can turn it to *blysse*.

15   '. . . the two visions of man, comic and tragic, merge together, both remaining within the temporal, both adumbrating the eternal' (Tristram, p. 32).

ABBREVIATIONS

CFMA	Classiques Français du Moyen Age
EETS	Early English Text Society
EETS ES	Early English Text Society, Extra Series
ELH	*ELH: A Journal of English Literary History*
FMLS	*Forum for Modern Language Studies*
GGK	*Sir Gawain and the Green Knight*
JEGP	*Journal of English and Germanic Philology*
ME	Middle English
MED	*Middle English Dictionary*, ed. H. Kurath, S. M. Kuhn, J. Reidy (Ann Arbor, Mich., 1952–)
Med. Aev.	*Medium Aevum*
MLQ	*Modern Language Quarterly*
MLR	*Modern Language Review*
MS	*Medieval Studies*
Neophil.	*Neophilologus*
N&Q	*Notes and Queries*
NM	*Neuphilologische Mitteilungen*
NMS	*Nottingham Medieval Studies*
OE	Old English
OED	*The Oxford English Dictionary*, ed. Sir J. A. H. Murray, H. Bradley, Sir W. Craigie, C. T. Onions (Oxford, 1933)
SP	*Studies in Philology*
STS	Scottish Text Society
TGD	*Sir Gawain and the Green Knight*, ed. J. R. R. Tolkien and E. V. Gordon, second edition, revised N. Davis (Oxford, 1967)

BIBLIOGRAPHY

Ackerman, R. W., 'Gawain's Shield: Penitential Doctrine in *GGK*', *Anglia* 76 (1958), 254–65.

Barron, W. R. J., *GGK*, ed. and trans. (Manchester, 1974).

Barron W. R. J. (1973), 'French Romance and the Structure of *GGK*', in *Studies in Medieval Literature and Language in Memory of Frederick Whitehead*, ed. Rothwell, Barron, Blamires, Thorpe (Manchester, 1973), 7–25.

Barron, W. R. J. (1978), 'A propos de quelques cas d'écorchement dans les romans anglais et français du Moyen Age', in *Mélanges Jeanne Lods* (Paris, 1978), 49–68.

Benson, L. D., *Art and Tradition in 'GGK'* (New Brunswick, N.J., 1965).

Bercovitch, S., 'Romance and Anti-Romance in *GGK*', *Philological Quarterly* 44 (1965), 30–7.

Blanch, R. J., 'Games Poets Play: The Ambiguous Use of Colour Symbolism in *GGK*', *NMS* 20 (1976), 64–85.

Brewer, D. S., 'Courtesy and the *Gawain*-Poet', in *Patterns of Love and Courtesy: Essays in Memory of C. S. Lewis*, ed. Lawlor (London, 1966), 54–85.

Brewer, D. S. (1967), 'The *Gawain*-Poet: A General Appreciation of the Four Poems', *Essays in Criticism* 17 (1967), 130–42.

Burnley, J. D., 'The Hunting Scenes in *GGK*', *The Yearbook of English Studies* 3 (1973), 1–9.

Burrow, J. A., *A Reading of 'GGK'* (London, 1965).

Butturff, D. R., 'Laughter and Discovered Aggression in *GGK*', *Literature and Psychology* 22 (1972), 139–47.

Carson, Mother A., 'Morgain la Fée as the Principle of Unity in *GGK*', *MLQ* 23 (1962), 3–16.

Cawley, A. C., *Pearl, GGK*, ed. (London, 1962).

Champion, L. C., 'Grace versus Merit in *GGK*', *MLQ* 28 (1967), 413–25.

Christmas, P., 'A Reading of *GGK*', *Neophil.* 58 (1974), 238–47.

Davenport, W. A., *The Art of the 'Gawain'-Poet* (London, 1978).

David, A., 'Gawain and Aeneas', *English Studies* 49 (1968), 402–9.

Delaney, P., 'The Role of the Guide in *GGK*', *Neophil.* 49 (1965), 250–5.

Dickins, B., 'The Nine Unworthies', in *Medieval Literature and Civilization: Studies in Memory of G. N. Garmonsway*, ed. Pearsall and Waldron (London, 1969), 228–32.

Donner, M., 'Tact as a Criterion of Reality in *GGK*', *Papers in English Language and Literature* 1 (1965), 306–15.

Eadie, J., 'Morgain la Fée and the Conclusion of *GGK*', *Neophil.* 52 (1968), 299–304.

Engelhardt, G. J., 'The Predicament of Gawain', *MLQ* 16 (1955), 218–25.

Evans, W. O., 'The Case for Sir Gawain Re-opened', *MLR* 68 (1973), 721–33.

Field, P. J. C., 'A Re-reading of *GGK*', *SP* 68 (1971), 255–69.

Foley, M. M., 'Gawain's Two Confessions Reconsidered', *The Chaucer Review* 9 (1974–5), 73–9.

Gallant, G., 'The Three Beasts: Symbols of Temptation in *GGK*', *Annuale Mediaevale* 11 (1970), 35–50.

Gardner, J., *The Complete Works of the 'Gawaian'-Poet*, trans. (Chicago, 1965).

Goldhurst, W., 'The Green and the Gold: The Major Theme of *GGK*', *College English* 20 (1958–9), 61–5.

Gollancz, Sir I., *GGK*, ed., EETS 210 (London, 1940).

Green, D. H., 'Irony and Medieval Romance', *FMLS* 6 (1970), 49–64.

Green, R. H., 'Gawain's Shield and the Quest for Perfection', *ELH* 29 (1962), 121–39, reprinted in *'Sir Gawain' and 'Pearl': Critical Essays*, ed. Blanch (Bloomington, Ind., 1966).

Gross, L., 'Gawain's Acceptance of the Girdle', *American Notes and Queries* 12 (1973–4), 154–5.

Haines, V. Y., 'Allusions to the *felix culpa* in the Prologue of *GGK*', *Revue de l'Université d'Ottawa* 44 (1974), 158–77.

Haines, V. Y. (1976), 'When Gawain Sins', *Revue de l'Université d'Ottawa* 46 (1976), 242–6.

Henry, A., 'Temptation and Hunt in *GGK*', *Med. Aev.* 45 (1976), 187–99.

Hieatt, A. K., '*GGK*: pentangle, *luf-lace*, numerical structure', in *Silent Poetry: Essays in Numerological Analysis*, ed. Fowler (London, 1970), 116–40.

Howard, D. R., *The Three Temptations: Medieval Man in Search of the World* (Princeton, N.J., 1966).

Hughes, D. W., 'The Problem of Reality in *GGK*', *University of Toronto Quarterly* 40 (1970–1), 217–35.

Hunt, T., 'Gawain's Fault and the Moral Perspectives of *GGK*', *Trivium* 10 (1975), 1–18.

Hunt, T. (1976), 'Irony and Ambiguity in *GGK*', *FMLS* 12 (1976), 1–16.

Jacobs, N., 'Gawain's False Confession', *English Studies* 51 (1970), 433–5.

Käsmann, H., 'Numerical Structure in Fitt III of *GGK*', in *Chaucer and Middle English Studies in Honour of Rossell Hope Robbins*, ed. Rowland (London, 1974), 131–9.

Kittredge, G. L., *A Study of GGK* (Cambridge, Mass., 1916).

Lester, G. A., 'Gawain's Fault in Terms of Contemporary Law of Arms', *N&Q* 221 (1976), 392–3.

Longo, J. A., '*GGK*: The Christian Quest for Perfection', *NMS* 11 (1967), 57–85.

Loomis, R. S., *Wales and the Arthurian Legend* (Cardiff, 1956).

Loomis, R. S. (1963), *The Development of Arthurian Romance* (London, 1963).

McAlindon, T., 'Comedy and Terror in Middle English Literature', *MLR* 60 (1965), 323–32.

McClure,P., 'Gawain's *mesure* and the Significance of the Three Hunts in *GGK*', *Neophil.* 57 (1973), 375–87.

Margeson, R. W., 'Structure and Meaning in *GGK*', *Papers on Language and Literature* 13 (1977), 16–24.

Mehl, D., *The Middle English Romances of the Thirteenth and Fourteenth Centuries* (London, 1969).

Mills, D., 'An Analysis of the Temptation Scenes in *GGK*', *JEGP* 67 (1968), 612–30.

Mills, D. (1970), 'The Rhetorical Function of Gawain's Antifeminism', *NM* 71 (1970), 635–40.

Mills, M., 'Christian Significance and Romance Tradition in *GGK*', *MLR* 60 (1965), 483–93.

Moon, D. M., 'The Role of Morgain la Fée in *GGK*', *NM* 67 (1966), 31–57.

Pearsall, D. A., 'Rhetorical "Descriptio" in *GGK*', *MLR* 50 (1955), 129–34.

Pierle, R. C., '*GGK*: A Study in Moral Complexity', *The Southern Quarterly* 6 (1967–8), 203–11.

Randall, D. B. J., 'Was the Green Knight a Fiend?', *SP* 57 (1960), 479–91.

Renoir, A., 'An Echo to the Sense: The Patterns of Sound in *GGK*', *English Miscellany* 13 (1962), 9–23.

Savage, H. L., *The 'Gawain'-Poet: Studies in his Personality and Background* (Chapel Hill, N.C., 1956).

Schnyder, H., *GGK: An Essay in Interpretation* (Berne, 1961).

Shedd, G. M., 'The Knight in Tarnished Armour: The Meaning of *GGK*', *MLR* 62 (1967), 3–13.

Silverstein, T., 'The Art of *GGK*', *University of Toronto Quarterly* 33 (1963–4), 258–78.

Smithers, G. V., 'What *GGK* is About', *Med. Aev.* 32 (1963), 171–89.

Spearing, A.C., *The 'Gawain'-Poet: A Critical Study* (Cambridge, 1970).

Spendal, R. J., 'The Fifth Pentad in *GGK*', *N&Q* 221 (1976), 147–8.

Stevens, M., 'Laughter and Game in *GGK*', *Speculum* 47 (1972), 65–78.

Tamplin, R., 'The Saints in *GGK*', *Speculum* 44 (1969), 403–20.

Taylor, P. B. (1969), '"Blysse and blunder", Nature and Ritual in *GGK*', *English Studies* 50 (1969), 165–75.

Taylor, P. B., 'Commerce and Comedy in *GGK*', *Philological Quarterly* 50 (1971), 1–15.

Thiébaux, M., *The Stag of Love: The Chase in Medieval Literature* (Ithaca, N.Y., 1974).

Thiébaux, M. (1970), 'Sir Gawain, the Fox Hunt, and Henry of Lancaster', *NM* 71 (1970), 469–79.

Tristram, P., *Figures of Life and Death in Medieval English Literature* (London, 1976).

Turville-Petre, T., *The Alliterative Revival* (Cambridge, 1977).
Waldron, R. A. *GGK* ed. (London, 1970).
Whiting, B. J., 'Gawain: His Reputation, His Courtesy and His Appearance in Chaucer's *Squire's Tale*', *Medieval Studies* 9 (1947), 189–234.
Wilson, E., *The 'Gawain'-Poet* (Leiden, 1976).

PUBLICATIONS
OF THE FACULTY OF ARTS,
UNIVERSITY OF MANCHESTER

The following are still available:

K. M. T. Chrimes, *The 'Respublica Lacedaemoniorum' ascribed to Xenophon*. No 1, 1948.

J. M. H. Gautier, *L'Exotisme américain dans l'œuvre de Chateaubriand: étude de vocabulaire*. No 4, 1951.

H. D. Westlake, *Timoleon and his relations with tyrants*. No 5, 1952.

R. B. Tate, *Joan Margarit i Pau, Cardinal Bishop of Gerona*. No 6, 1955.

M. Wallenstein, *Some unpublished piyyutim from the Cairo Genizah*. No 7, 1957.

D. M. White, *Zaccaria Seriman: the 'Viaggi di Enrico Wanton': a contribution to the study of the Enlightenment in Italy*. No 12, 1961.

H. Ramsden, *Weak-pronoun position in the early Romance languages*. No 14, 1963.

D. M. MacDowell, *Athenian homicide law in the age of the orators*. No 15, 1963.

I. Michael, *The treatment of classical material in the 'Libro de Alexandre'*. No 17, 1970.

D. G. M. McArthur, *Les Constructions verbales du francais contemporain: une description des fonctions*. No 18, 1971.

S. Ralphs, *Dante's journey to the centre: some patterns in his allegory*. No 19, 1972.

R. Hastings, *Nature and reason in the 'Decameron'*. No 21, 1975.

B. M. Ratcliffe and W. H. Chaloner, *A French sociologist looks at Britain: Gustave d'Eichthal and British society in 1828*. No 22, 1977.

J. N. Adams, *The Vulgar Latin of the letters of Claudius Terentianus*. No 23, 1977.

D. Blamires, *Herzog Ernst and the otherworld voyage: a comparative study*. No 24, 1979.

W. R. J. Barron, *Trawthe and treason: the sin of Gawain reconsidered*. No 25, 1980.